A TRADERS HANDBOOK

THE REVERSAL DAY PHENOMENON

By John Crane

Tradenet Publishing Company
Loveland, Colorado

ISBN # 188 3272 289

Printed in the United States of America

All charts used in this manual are furnished courtesy of FutureSource TM
All charts used for examples are from 1996.

Disclaimer

It should not be assumed that the methods, techniques, or indicators presented in this book will be profitable or that they will not result in losses. Past results are not necessarily indicative of future results. Examples in this book are for educational purposes only. This is not a solicitation of any order to buy or sell.

The NFA requires us to state that "HYPOTHETICAL OR SIMULATED PERFORMANCE RESULTS HAVE CERTAIN INHERENT LIMITATIONS. UNLIKE AN ACTUAL PERFORMANCE RECORD, SIMULATED RESULTS DO NOT REPRESENT ACTUAL TRADING. ALSO, SINCE THE TRADES HAVE NOT ACTUALLY BEEN EXECUTED, THE RESULTS MAY HAVE UNDER OR OVERCOMPENSATED FOR THE IMPACT, IF ANY, OF CERTAIN MARKET FACTORS, SUCH AS LACK OF LIQUIDITY. SIMULATED TRADING PROGRAMS IN GENERAL ARE ALSO SUBJECT TO THE FACT THAT THEY ARE DESIGNED WITH THE BENEFIT OF HINDSIGHT. NO REPRESENTATION IS BEING MADE THAT ANY ACCOUNT WILL OR IS LIKELY TO ACHIEVE PROFITS OR LOSSES SIMILAR TO THOSE SHOWN.

CONTENTS

CONTENTS
continued

To my wife, Angela, and my two daughters, Ana and Holli, who never let me forget what is really important in life.

And

To may father and mother, for their unwavering love and support.

Chapter 1

INTRODUCTION

I opened the seminar with this shocker. "I can predict the future. In fact, all of us are capable of seeing into the future."

A few attendees chuckled nervously, but most glared with great skepticism. Undaunted, I pulled out a calendar. "With this tool, I can tell the exact date of the next full moon."

As I continued, their expression cleared and amazement replaced confusion. "I know the exact time of today's sunset, and tomorrow's sunrise by using an almanac. I also know when the tide will rise and ebb, what the temperature in my state will average...In short, I can foretell the future. "

I then asked the audience to give me examples of predictions. Some of the answers, such as the appearance of certain stars in the sky, we accepted as completely reliable. Others, such as determining the next flu epidemic, were considered risky.

So, what makes us comfortable with a prediction? The group decided that the credibility of the source was very important. A trusted 'expert' must back up his prediction with facts, documentation and historical evidence. It also helps if the ordinary person understands the reasoning behind the prediction. The Commodity Market has its experts as well. Technical analysts 'study' the markets and, based upon their historical observations, devise methods to predict its future.

Unfortunately, many of these 'experts' lose credibility due to their cumbersome or questionable methods. However, once in a while, an expert will come along with a simple, reliable method, and the entire world of commodities will hunger after his secret...such was a man named WD Gann.

Before his death in 1954, Gann reputedly made as much as $50 million trading the markets. His ability to pinpoint the *exact* turning point in the futures market was unparalleled and legendary. For instance, he predicted the 1929 stock market crash...a full nine months before it occurred. In 1932, he foretold that the market would hit a low six months before it occurred!

Yet, his most famous and uncanny prediction occurred in 1909. On September 21 of that year, Gann predicted that the September wheat would trade at $1.20 a bushel *on or before* September 30. At the time, wheat was struggling at $1.05.

When September 30 arrived (the contract expiration date) September wheat had not moved above $1.08. In fact it remained almost stagnant for the entire day.

When confronted with this apparent error, Gann stubbornly folded his arms across his chest and stated, "If it does not touch $1.20 before the market closes, it will prove that there is something wrong with my whole method of calculations. I do not care what the price is now. It must go to $1.20."

Just minutes before the contract expired, the September wheat suddenly flew up to $1.20. Incredibly, it *closed at that price*!

What was WD Gann's famous reaction when questioned about this stunning forecast? "***The future is nothing but a repetition of the past. Everything moves in cycles as a result of the natural law of action and reaction.***"

Since then, many analysts have rewritten, rediscovered or redefined the methods of great traders such as Gann, Elliot or Fibonacci. Most of those so called *new discoveries*, however, are just *old techniques* with a few complicated bells and whistles added. They end up disappearing as quickly as they arrive. Why?

Most techniques only work under certain market conditions. For instance, one system may work well if the market is trending, but it collapses when the market turns sideways. A technique may be very profitable in bull markets, but will completely fail in a bear market. Some systems need breakouts with a strong follow through, and some need steady quiet markets.

Consequently, technical traders are always searching for that *one proven technique that adjusts to any market condition*...

We call it the *Reversal Day Technique.* It is primarily based on Gann's *action-reaction* theory but combines price levels, timing methods and confirmation patterns to strengthen the predictability.

We believe the search is over. Our flexible trading technique works well as a stand alone approach, yet incorporates with other trading methods. It is simple to implement, yet accurate enough to pinpoint timing signals. Best of all, this technique does not require large investment capital.

This allows the trader to see the market reaction long before it occurs. In fact, once these three elements harmonize, the most amazing and precise trading signals occur!

Let's prove our point with the September Copper chart on page 8.

With our technique, we spotted May 13 as a Reversal Day two weeks before it occurred. Look at the example on the next page. Notice how the market began a free fall (3630 points) ***the day after*** we predicted a date! Traders coming into this market could have earned over $9,000!

The price plunged because of reported company losses and improper trading practices. However, the Reversal Day Technique predicted the drop *before* the *reasons* behind the fall became public knowledge.

Are you beginning to see the potential? If not, we'll give you another example.

September Copper

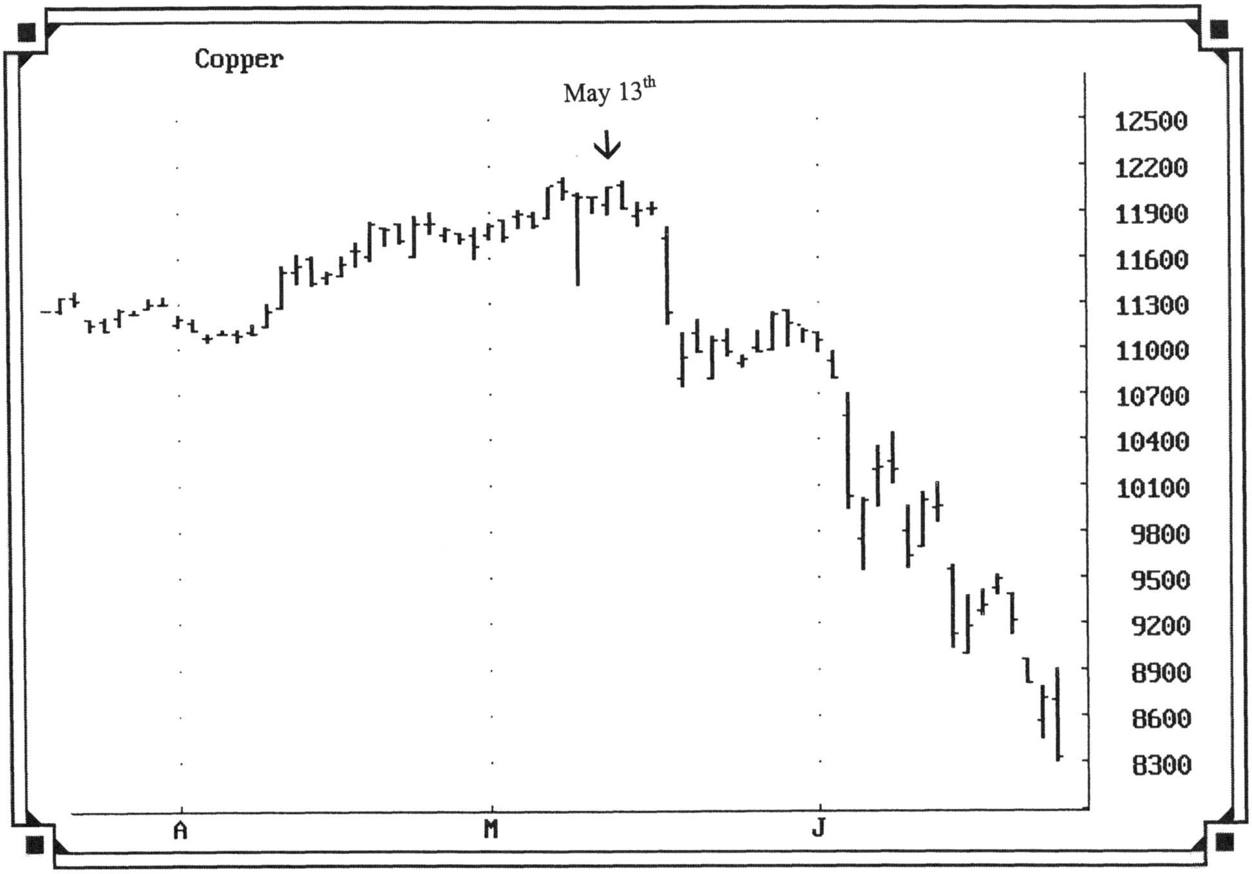

In this second example we use a graph to dramatically display the effectiveness of our technique.

Here we forecasted the Reversal Date of January 3rd for the June Treasury Bonds. After this sell signal the T-Bond market never looked back as it traded lower over the next six months. The major moved ended on another forecasted Reversal Date, June 14th. Think what you could do with this powerful tool at your disposal every day!

We hope that you are beginning to catch our enthusiasm for this technique. Those who witness the reliability of the Reversal Day Technique itch to invest. What's more, this technique does not require that you disrupt your regular schedule in order to monitor your trades.

However, telling people about the Reversal Day Technique is one thing... getting them comfortable enough to use it is another. Therefore, we wrote this book with one objective... compose it in such a manner that anyone can replicate the lessons. The next few pages describe the means by which we teach our technique.

June T-Bonds

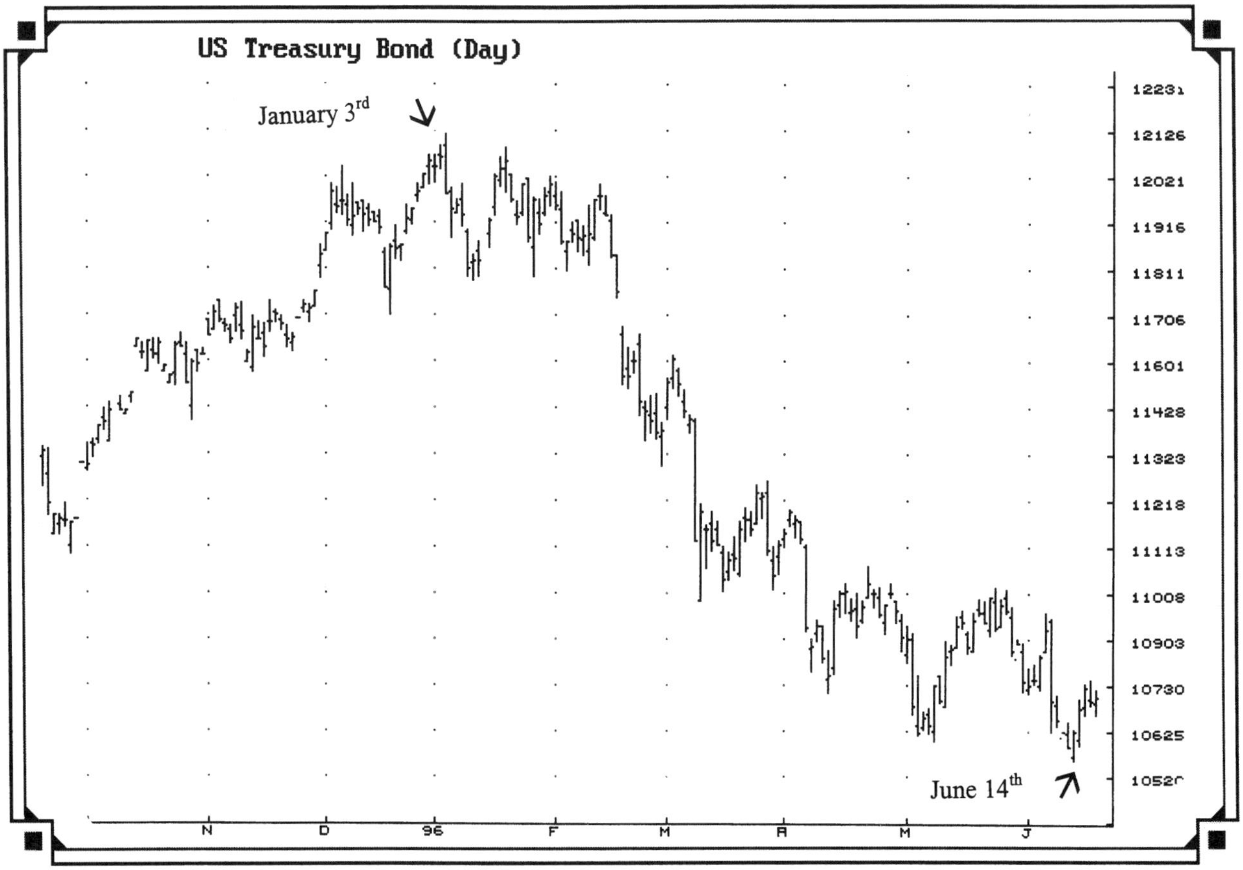
US Treasury Bond (Day)
January 3rd
June 14th
12231
12126
12021
11916
11811
11706
11601
11428
11323
11218
11113
11008
10903
10730
10625
10520
N
D
96
F
M
A
M
J

Leading Indicators

Technical indicators, such as moving averages, relative strength index, stochastics, etc., help predict future markets through *lagging indicators*. Unfortunately, these indicators do not signal a buy until *after* a majority of the *price move is over*. Similarly, breakout methods may lead the trader into overbought or oversold markets. General cycles often bottom too early or too late in long and short term cycles. None are acceptable for reliable analysis.

On the other hand, our method looks to *leading indicators* to signal Reversal dates. Included are reversal patterns, continuation patterns, major and minor buy/sell windows, and support and resistance formations. All of these have one purpose: get you into the market *at the beginning* of the trend where profits are greater. This book devotes considerable time explaining how to use *leading indicators with Reversal Days.*

Charts and Graphs

As you saw in the previous two examples, pictures tell their own story. That is why we use extensive charts and graphs throughout this book. Charts not only reinforce our point, but help you to better understand the necessary principles and calculations. This book is loaded with examples. We hope you use them frequently.

Price Patterns and Timing Strategies

Even if you have never invested before, the lessons on price patterns and timing will build your confidence.

Rules And Summaries for a Trading Plan

We have summarized most chapters with a *What You Should Know* page. We think this summary sheet will not only help as a learning tool, but also as a quick reference in the future. Ultimately, we believe these summaries will build confidence and hasten the learning time.

Definitions

We want every trader, no matter how experienced, to enjoy this book. Several times we pause and define terms as a way of review. This is a great resource for traders of all levels.

Money Management

No trading approach or timing strategy is correct 100% of the time. If you think otherwise, disappointment will soon be at your door. Our motto is: ***All Good Money Management Methods Come To The Aid Of Their Trader.***

We tell you everything you need to know about the critical management of investment funds including: how to make a good management plan, how to achieve money discipline, and how to stay detached from emotion. We also give extensive detail on where to place protective stops.

Paper Trading and Charting

Though the Reversal Day timing is uncanny, the trader must recognize and react to those signals. The one sure way to achieve this goal is to do homework in the form of charting and paper trading (tracking a market without investing)! We challenge you to find any chart and apply it to the Reversal Day Technique and see for yourself how frequently the Reversal Day Technique predicts the market turns.

We believe in our strategies, technique and methods. However, we know that if you consistently chart and paper trade, we will *prove it* to you. Therefore, we have devoted two chapters to help you get started.

In summary,

By the end of this book you should:

- *Spot a Reversal Day opening*
- *Predict future Reversal dates*
- *Identify Confirmation Patterns*
- *Determine correct Buy and Sell price levels*

Chapter 2

HISTORY REPEATS ITSELF

There are two primary methods of price forecasting: *fundamental* and *technical.* We want to take a moment to tell you why we are strong advocates of technical analysis...

Fundamental Vs. Technical

A fundamental analyst uses the news and various reports to predict market direction. They want *reasons* for the rise or fall of a market and use traditional 'supply and demand' economics to make market decisions. For instance, fundamentalists will study weather forecasts, crop conditions and planted acres. Based upon those reports they will determine if the crop looks 'bullish' or 'bearish'.

On the other hand, a technical analyst studies the effect of a particular price movement within a market. They look for a historical trend before charting a course. Technical analysts, or chartists, don't concern themselves with reasons for the rise or fall of prices. Instead, they want to know how a charted pattern *historically* reacts to this rise or fall.

Why do we prefer this method? Some of the most dramatic bull and bear markets start with little or no change on the *fundamental* side of the market. Although frequently there are fundamental reasons behind market movements, it often takes time to catch up with the technical indicators and that means you may miss out on the beginning of a move.

Not so with Technical Investors. Price charts often flag technical traders of a move long *before* the reaction. For instance, a Fundamental trader may look at a climbing corn chart and say, "The market is climbing because of a drought in Iowa."

However, a Technical trader doesn't care *why* the market is moving. Instead of waiting for some kind of bullish report to confirm the trend, technical traders observe price movements. They are looking for a 'typical' pattern. Based on these historical fluctuations, the next move is mathematically calculated. Consequently, they often *see* the drought *before* it hits the newsstand. Some of the biggest market movements occur long before the publication of confirming reports.

This concept often confuses fundamental traders and so they wait for the publication of a report before trading. These traders think the report will *cause* the market to move. Unfortunately, these unlucky traders will not get in until the end of that move. Why?

There is an old market saying, "Buy the Rumor and Sell the Fact." This is how it works. Let's say there is a report due out in a week or two. The *rumor is bullish* and so smart traders use that information to buy the market. Consequently, the market will, most likely, rise on the ***anticipation*** *of a bullish market.*

Now let's say that the report came out and the rumor of a bullish market proves true. Usually, the market reacts by opening higher, but may quickly run out of steam. Those traders that came in *before* the report will look to sell and take their profits. This causes the market to sell off and move lower.

You may wonder why traders sell off with a bullish report. Remember, we are trading the *futures* markets. We trade on the anticipation of what the markets will do in three, six and nine months from now. We are not trading the *present* market (cash market). Once released, the future report actually becomes a *present* report. Tomorrow it will be a past report.

Once a future report becomes a present or past report it has little bearing on the futures prices. The only exception is when the report contains surprising information.

Are we saying that fundamental traders never profit? No, of course not. The larger, well-informed firms have the people and resources to watch for every news flash or obscure farm report. Consequently, they are able to predict a market with some success.

However, most of us don't have the time or desire to read page after page of hog reports before investing in Pork Bellies. For the small trader, the technical approach is the clearest way of predicting the futures.

There is one more reason why we prefer the technical approach. The fundamental traders, for all their research into 'current' events, basically guess what the future will do. They don't really *know* if the rumor of a civil war in Saudi Arabia will affect the price of crude oil...they are only guessing.

On the other hand, Technical traders are more calculating. Instead of future predictions, they look to historical market data. They study price charts. These patterns reveal the historical reaction of the market in a bullish situation (upward trend) as well as the bearish situation (downward trend). As a result, Technical traders often see a trend long before anyone prints reports or headlines.

Chapter 3

CHARTING THE WAY

All of our methods, patterns and strategies are rooted in charts. Therefore, even though this chapter may be a review, we think it is well worth your time to examine it. *Remember, for a technical trader, charting is your most important key to success...*

Why We Use Charts

The whole purpose of charting is to analyze the market action. This analysis aids the chartist in identifying trends (patterns) right from the beginning of a development.

Why is identifying the trend important? Trends are the roadmap for the market activity. Traders anticipate when the market will move and which direction it will go from the current trend. One of the most popular methods of determining the future trend is to refer to charts, both current and historical.

Bar Charts

Bar charts are the oldest and most popular method of graphing commodity prices because they are so simple to read. More importantly, for a technical trader, bar charts are easy to construct and maintain. The bar chart is the historical picture of the price action for a particular commodity. Often, we refer to this as the daily high, low and close chart. It contains a horizontal axis, which represents time, and a vertical axis which represents price.

What You Should Know About Bar Charts

Daily Bar Chart

In a daily chart, each bar represents one day of action. The daily record includes the 'high', 'low', and 'closing' prices. The vertical line will connect the high and the low (referred to as the 'range'). There is also a small horizontal bar (referred to as the 'tick') that represents the closing price. This bar will move one space to the right every day. *(See diagram on page 28).*

Weekly and Monthly Bar Charts

Statisticians know that the accuracy of an analysis increases with the length of a study. A daily bar chart goes back only about six months. However, the weekly chart can review up to five years of activity. The monthly chart sometimes traces 20 years. *(See diagram on page 29).* We use weekly and monthly bar charts to look at the 'big picture' of the price action. This compression of information helps us spot the longer-range trends.

Trends

Prices rarely move in a straight line. Instead, the market moves in one of three directions: up, down, or sideways. A trend occurs once a market movement establishes a noticeable pattern. Studying charts for even a brief moment demonstrates clearly that market activity usually moves in a trend. *(See diagrams on page 31-32)*

Major, Intermediate, Minor Trends

Charles H. Dow broke trends into three categories: The Major, the Intermediate and the Minor. The Major trend is in effect for more than one year; the intermediate trend lasts from three weeks to one month, and the minor lasts about three weeks. *(See diagram on page 35)*

Trend lines and Channels

The "trendline" and 'channel line' can be the most useful road map for predicting price movements. Let's review each.

Trendline

The trendline defincs thc 'slope' of the trend. Once this slope breaks, the alert sounds that the market may turnaround. It takes two points to draw a trendline and a third point to confirm the trend. We draw an *up trendline* under the successively higher reaction lows. We draw a *down trendline* above successively lower reaction highs. The trendline should touch the extreme high or low point of each reaction high or reaction low. (*See diagrams on pages 31-34)*

Channels

A *channel* occurs when the trend follows a straight line but parallel lines also appear over the reaction highs and under the reaction lows. Channels predetermine where the support and resistance will meet (*See diagrams on page 31-34)*.

Gaps

A *gap* is a space on the chart caused by a lack of trading. Generally, a gap signals a reversal trend. There are five identified kinds of gaps, several of which we will discuss in later chapters.

What You Should Know About Your Own Charting

1. *Acquiring Charts:* Before starting, you will need your own charts. These may be attained several different ways. For instance, there are charting companies that will send you updated charts every week. Computer programs are available which will download charts from different services. In addition, quote equipment may be acquired which updates any chart, any day, every minute.

2. *Chart the closest month to the current date*: During your training, we recommend you track *only the closest month* to the current date. These markets are usually the most liquid contract months, and therefore have the most volume and open interest.

3. *Don't trade in the Delivery Period:* If today was May 5 you would avoid May futures. May contracts would be in the *Delivery Period.* Instead, look for the *next* contract month available for that commodity.

4. *Different Delivery Months:* In most cases futures contracts do not trade every month. For instance, Wheat futures trade in March, May, July, September, and December.

Charting Terms:

Trend: *Price movement in a particular direction.*

Trend Lines: *Extreme moves toward the trend that connect together with a simple line. Duration and scope of the trendline are also important factors in determining pattern reliability. Normally, three trends will move simultaneously; the Minor, Intermediate and Major trend lines. A trader should be aware of the direction of the three trends before entering a trade.*

Minor Trend: *A trend that lasts for two days to four weeks. We recommend using a daily chart during a minor trend.*

Intermediate Trend: *A trend that ranges between four weeks to six months. We recommend a daily chart or weekly chart.*

Major Trend: *A trend that lasts from six months to five years. We recommend a monthly chart.*

Construction of a Trendline: *A minimum of two points connected together to 'test' a pattern. The validity of the prediction increases with the number of connected points.*

Upward trending market: *A line that extends to the lower side of a price and through the lowest lows. The highs will continue to get higher and the low will also trend higher. The trend line will go under the lows.*

Down trending Market: *The highs continue to get lower and the lows continue to get lower. The trend line will go above the market on the tops of highs.*

Channel: *The channel suggests a phase of over-bought and over-sold market conditions. It also helps determine a minor trend reversal. Long and short positions often reverse at the location of the channel lines. Draw parallel lines over the highs to see if channels form. One may connect two similar lows or two highs separated by at least two points, but the channel should not cross through any highs or lows.*

Risk: *We suggest placing a protective stop a point under the trendline for long trades and above the trendline for short trades.*

Gaps: *A gap is a space on the chart. The space occurs because there has been no trading for a period of time.*

Daily Bar Chart
Example 1

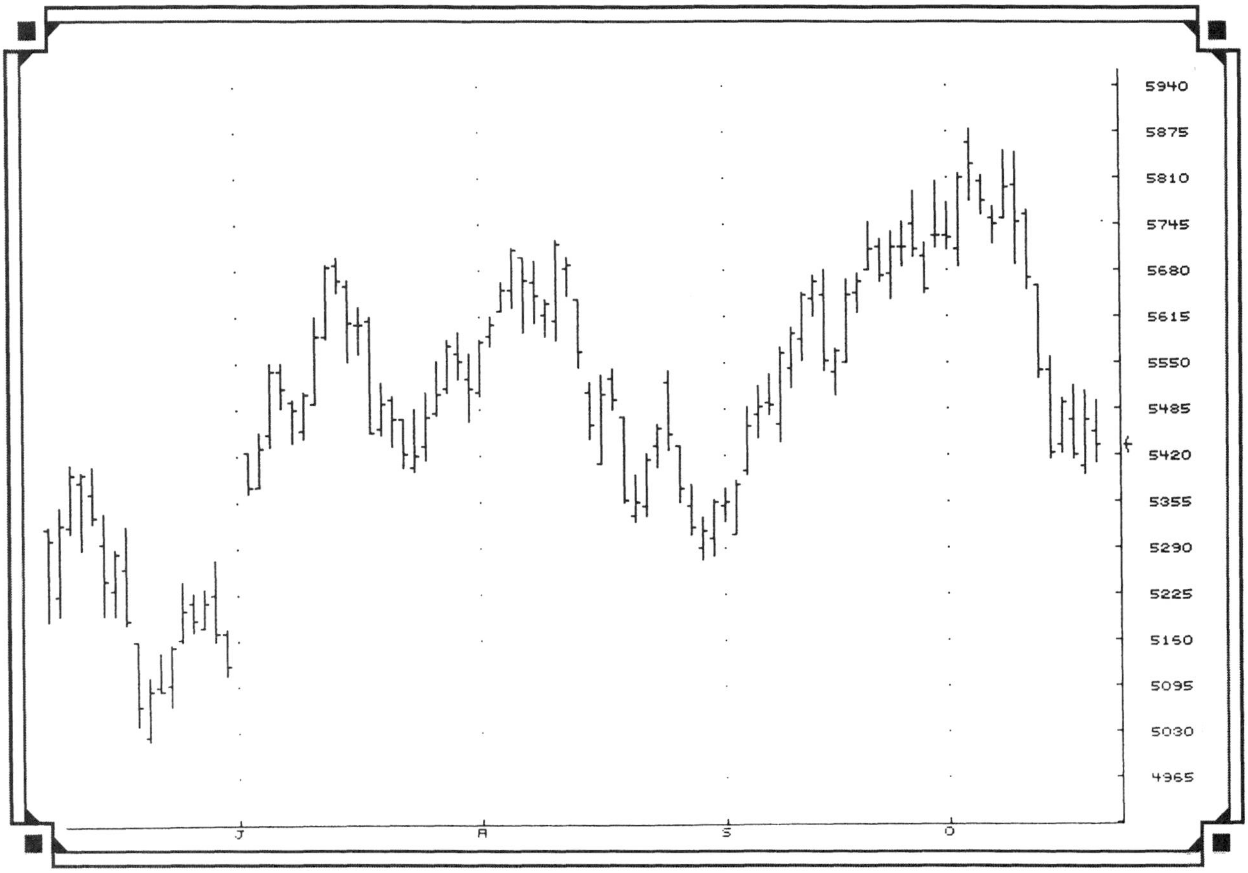

Daily charts identify short-term price movements.

Daily Charts Contain:

Vertical Line:	The price range of one day
High Point on Vertical:	High for that day
Low Point on Vertical:	Low for that day
Left side Hrz. Hash Mark:	Opening price
Right side Hrz. Hash Mark:	Closing price

Weekly Bar Chart

Example 1

Each vertical line represents one week

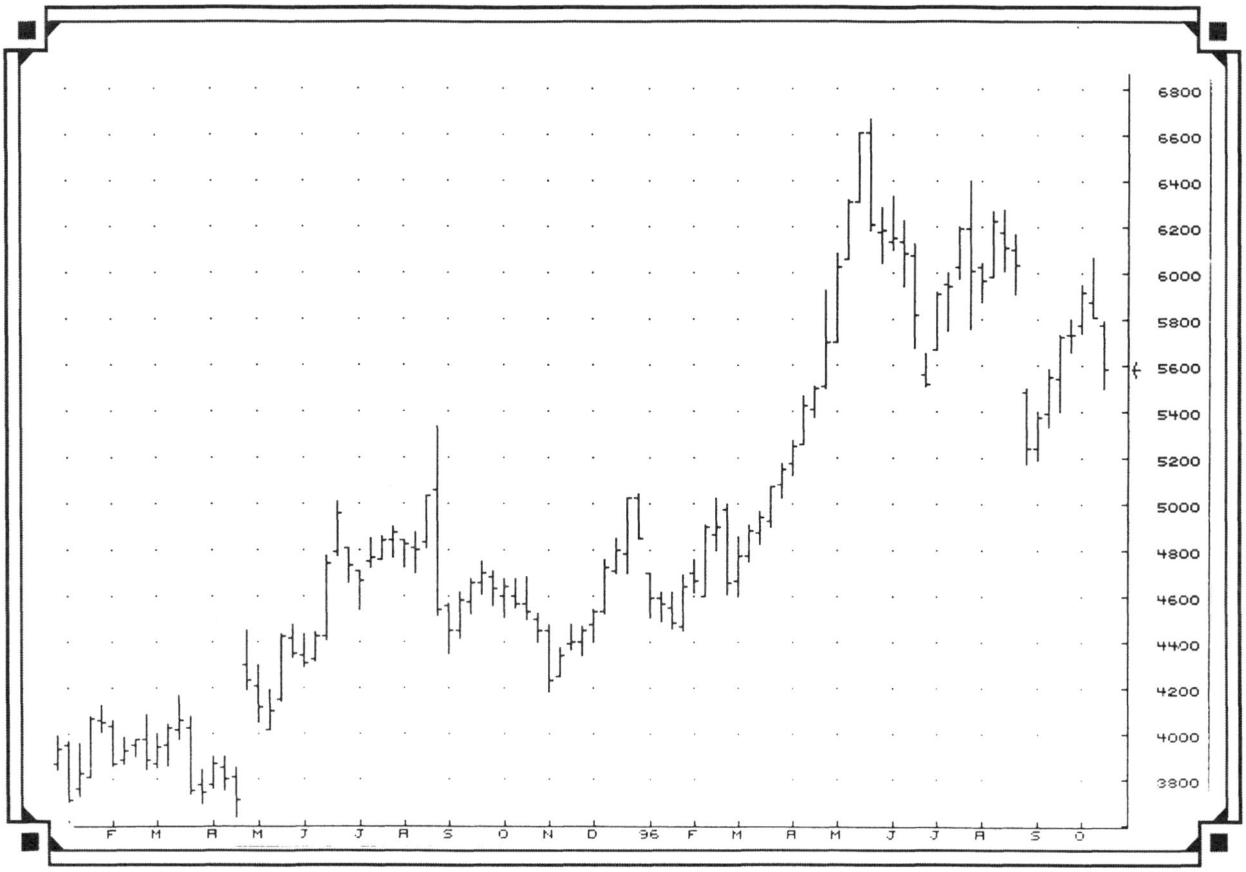

Weekly Charts show long term price movements

Monthly Bar Chart

Example 1

Each vertical line represents one month

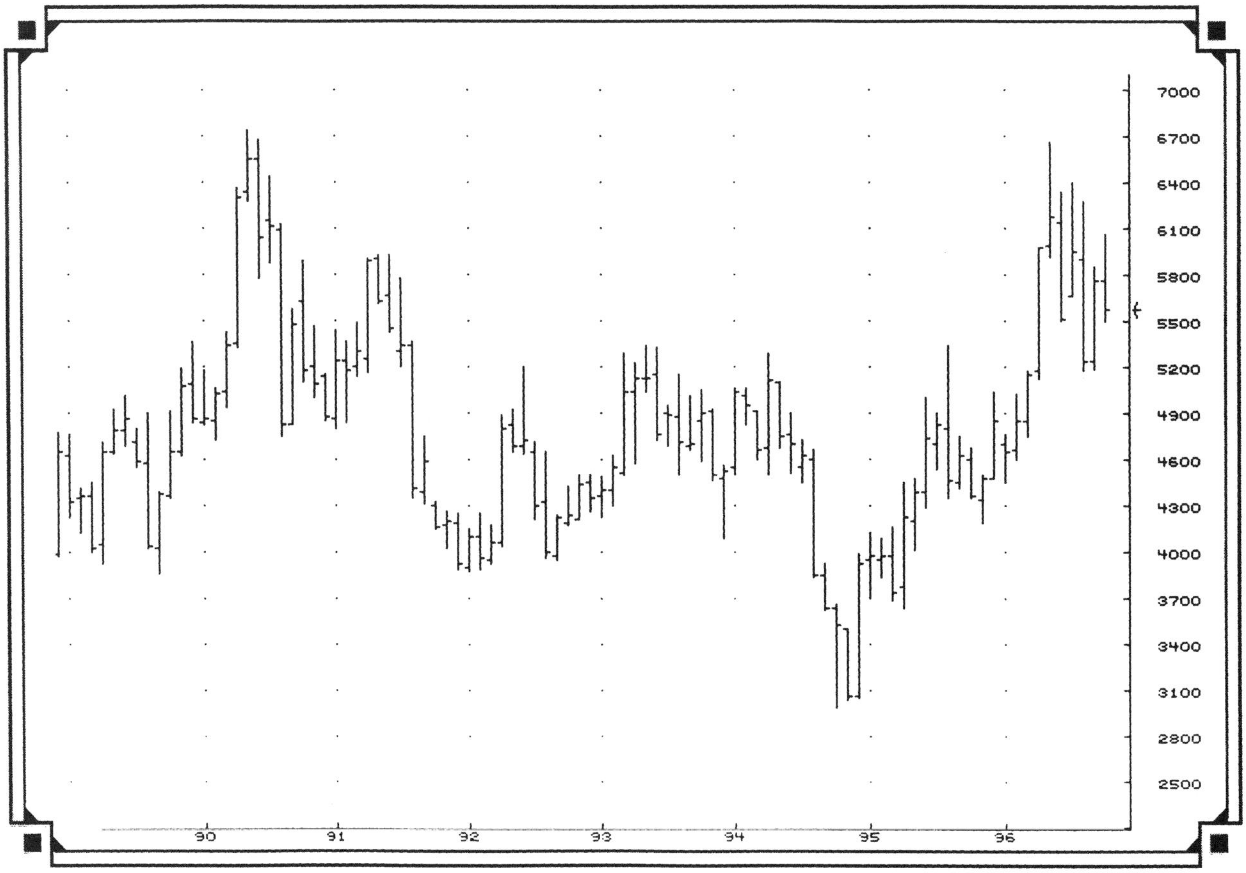

Monthly charts show longest term price movements

Trend Lines Off Of Highs
Example 1

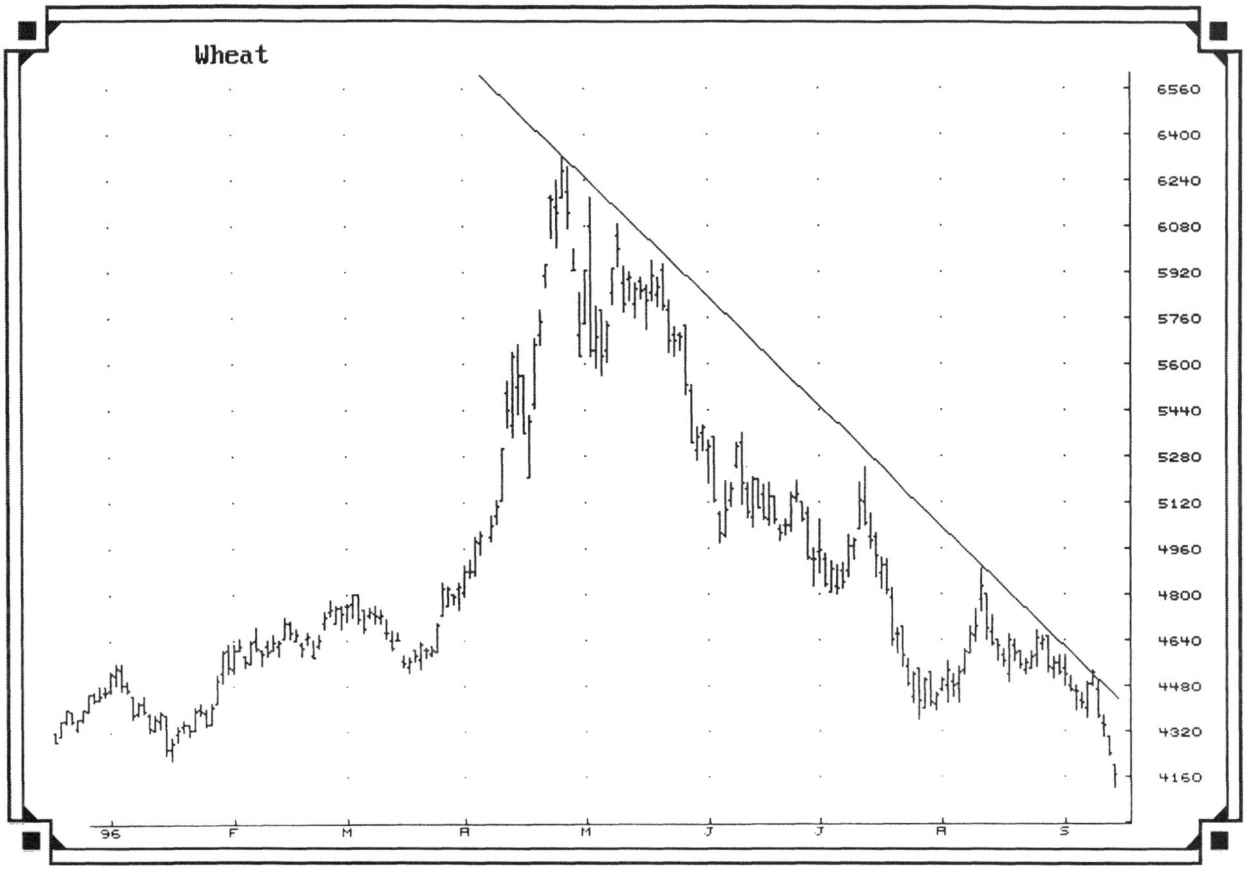

Trend Lines Off Of Lows
Example 1

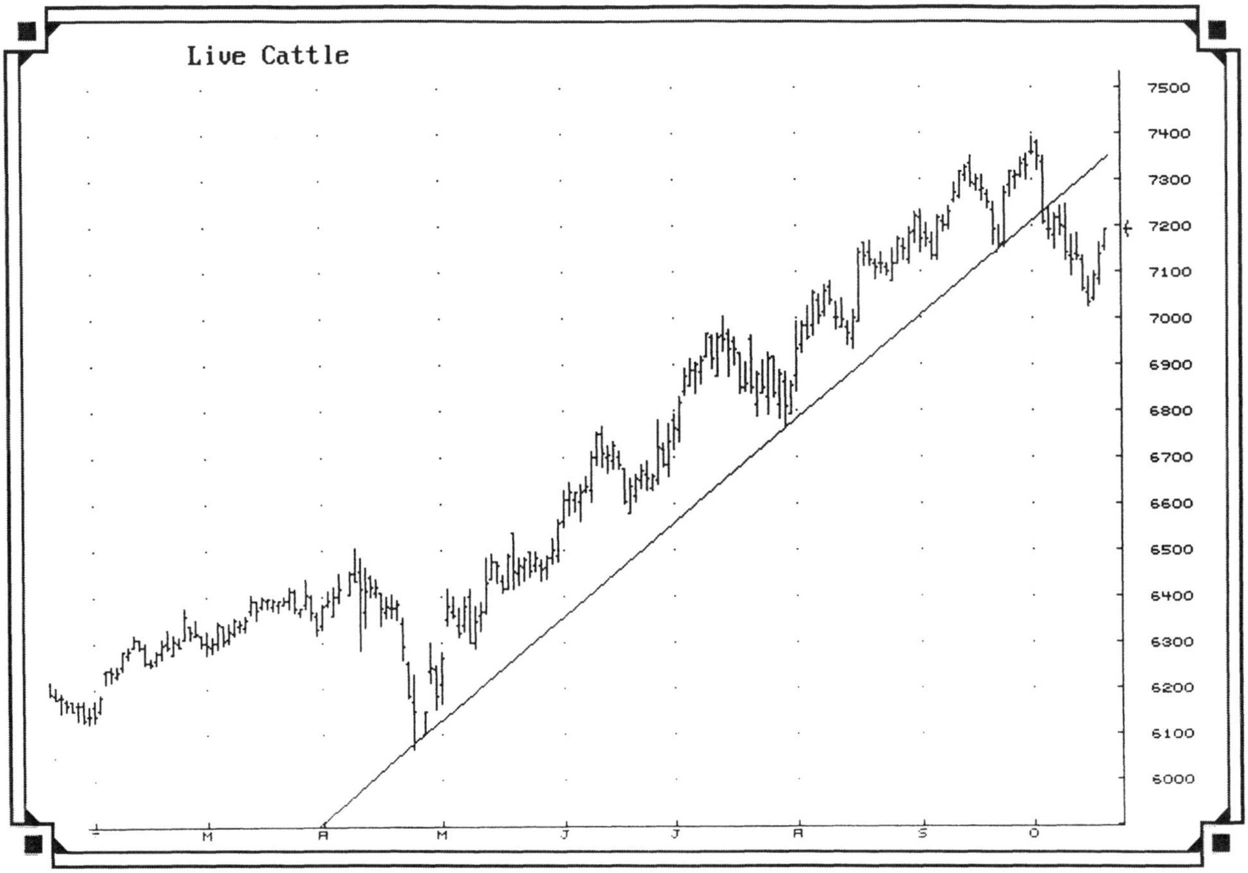

Bullish Channel Trend Lines
Example 1

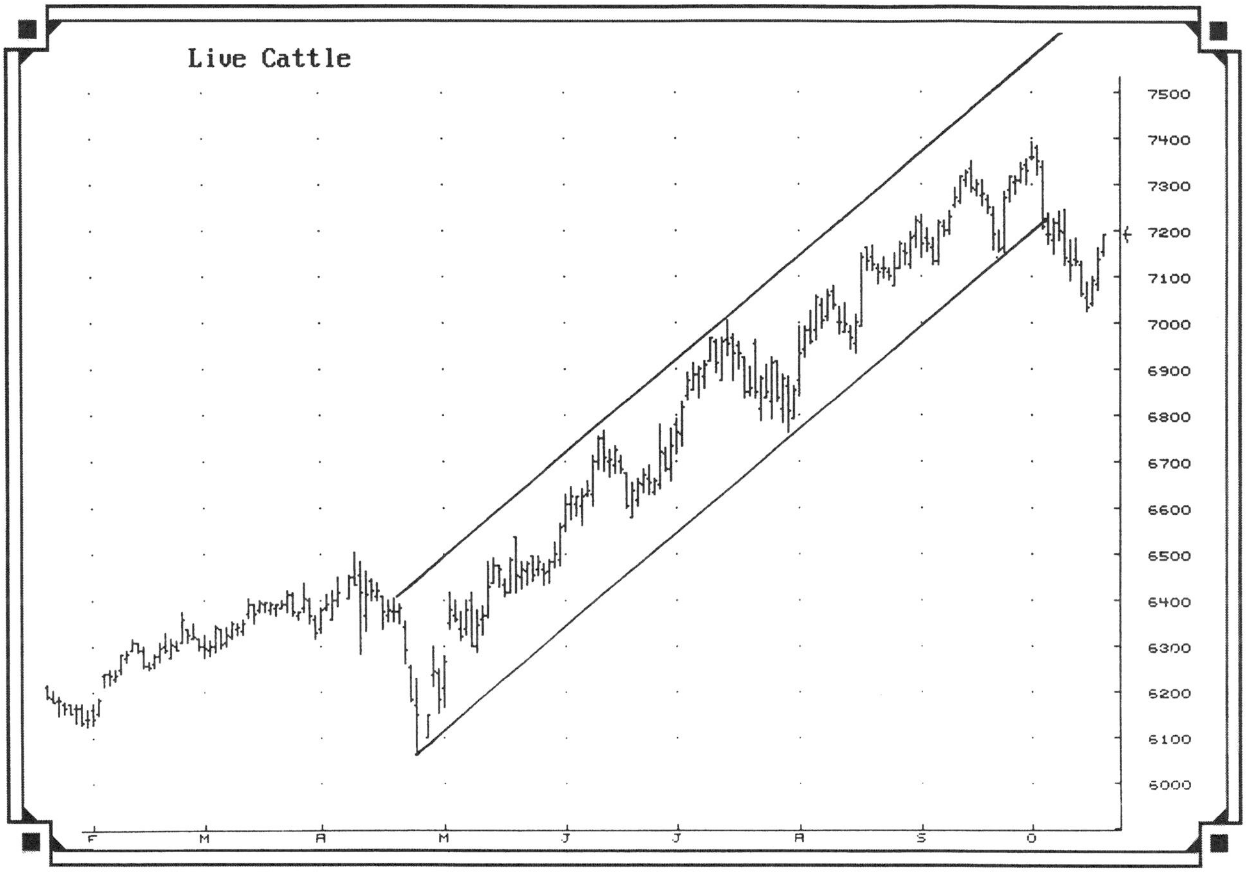

Bearish Channel Trend lines
Example 1

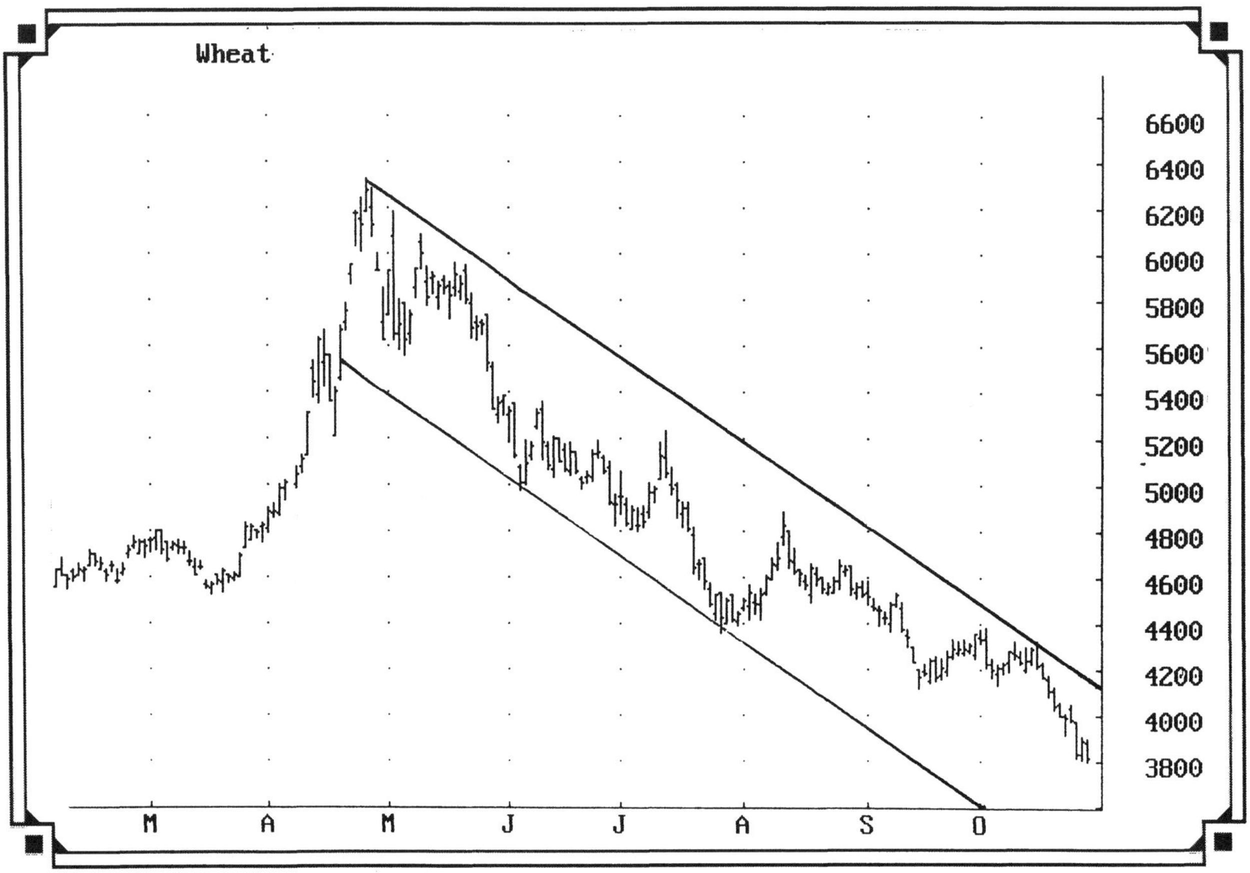

Minor, Intermediate, Major Trend Lines

Example 1

Chapter 4

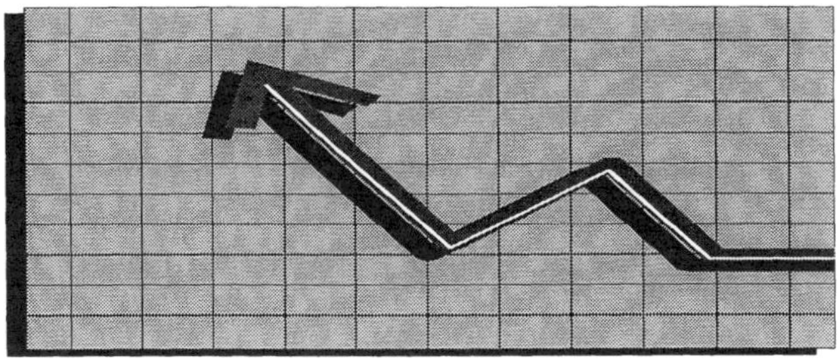

SUPPORT AND RESISTANCE

You will soon begin to notice that certain price levels attract buying (support) while others entice selling (resistance). In other words, knowing where the support and resistance levels are may help you determine your market entry and exit points.

This chapter defines support and resistance. You will learn where they are likely to occur, how they form, when to use them to place protective stops and how to target an area for taking profits before entering the market.

Supporting And Resisting

Support and Resistance are like a bend in the river. They are landmarks, if you will, of a good place to enter and a good place to exit. Even though the markets usually move in a wavelike motion with a series of highs and lows, they tend to *stop at historical highs and lows*. These highs and lows (peaks and troughs) are the *resistance and support* points.

The support and resistance levels come from *previous trading ranges*. If a particular commodity is trading in a range for a length of time, the range becomes symbolic and represents an idea of fair value for that time period. Once a level of support or resistance breaks, the market moves to the next level. It searches for a new fair price and a new level of support and resistance.

Traders find the market's *support and resistance* by studying past charts. For support, a chartist will note where, in the past, prices stopped *going down* and started moving up. This is *support. Resistance* occurs where the price started moving down. The *resistance level* occurs at the high.

Traders remember these levels through their charts. The longer the trading range lasts, the stronger the resistance. If prices begin to rise from this range, the old range becomes support.

Again, it is the *memory of the old range* as a fair market price that reinforces that attitude. Therefore, the *pullback to support,* or the return to the old range, becomes a good place to buy because of its history of fair market price. The more time spent in developing a support or resistance level the more powerful the level becomes.

A support and resistance congestion area may appear when prices trade within a certain range for several days or longer. These areas act as support when approached from above, or as resistance when approached from below. To determine the strength of a support or resistance congestion area, we study both the length of time and the volume of the price action activity.

Support/Resistance areas are divided into the following categories:

- *Major Support/Resistance*: The trading range occurs over six months and up.
- *Intermediate Support/Resistance*: The trading range occurs from 2 to 6 months.
- *Minor Support/Resistance*: The trading range occurs under 2 months.

What You Should Know About Support and Resistance

1. Support and Resistance are useful for locating entry and exit points.
   - Wait until the market drops to the support level on a commodity that you expect to go up (long position).
   - Look for rallies into the resistance levels on a commodity that you expect to go down (a short position).
2. Support and resistance levels help determine the location for stops.
   - Place a protective stop under the support area for a long position.
   - Place a protective stop above the resistance for a short position.
3. Penetration of support and resistance indicate the weakness or strength of the market.
   - A penetration of a support level indicates further weakness in the market.
   - A penetration of a resistance level indicates further strength in the market.
4. The support and resistance locations help define the risk.
   - Risk is the distance between the entry price and the stop point.
5. If the support and resistance areas are broken, they become the opposite.
   - Broken support becomes resistance and broken resistance becomes support.

Support And Resistance
Example 1

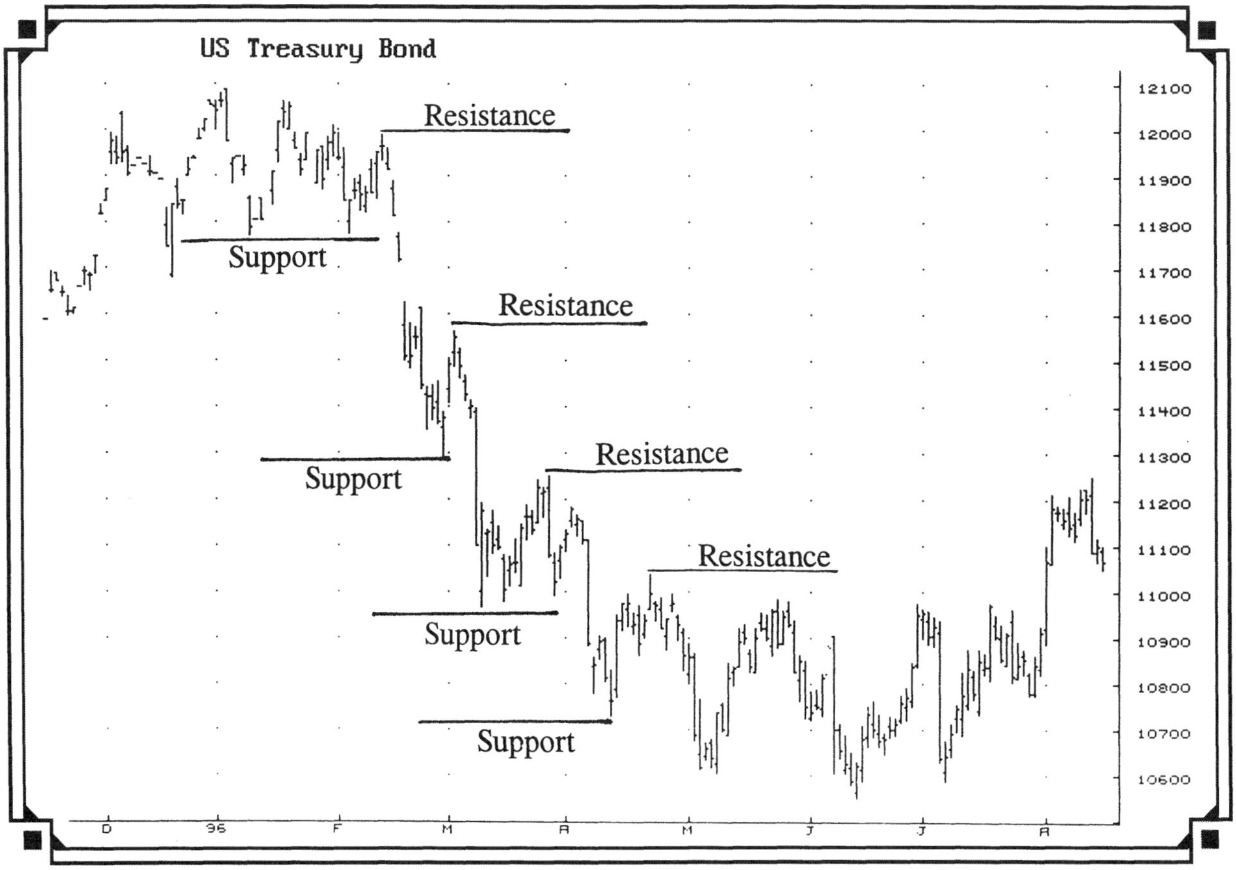

Support And Resistance
Example 2

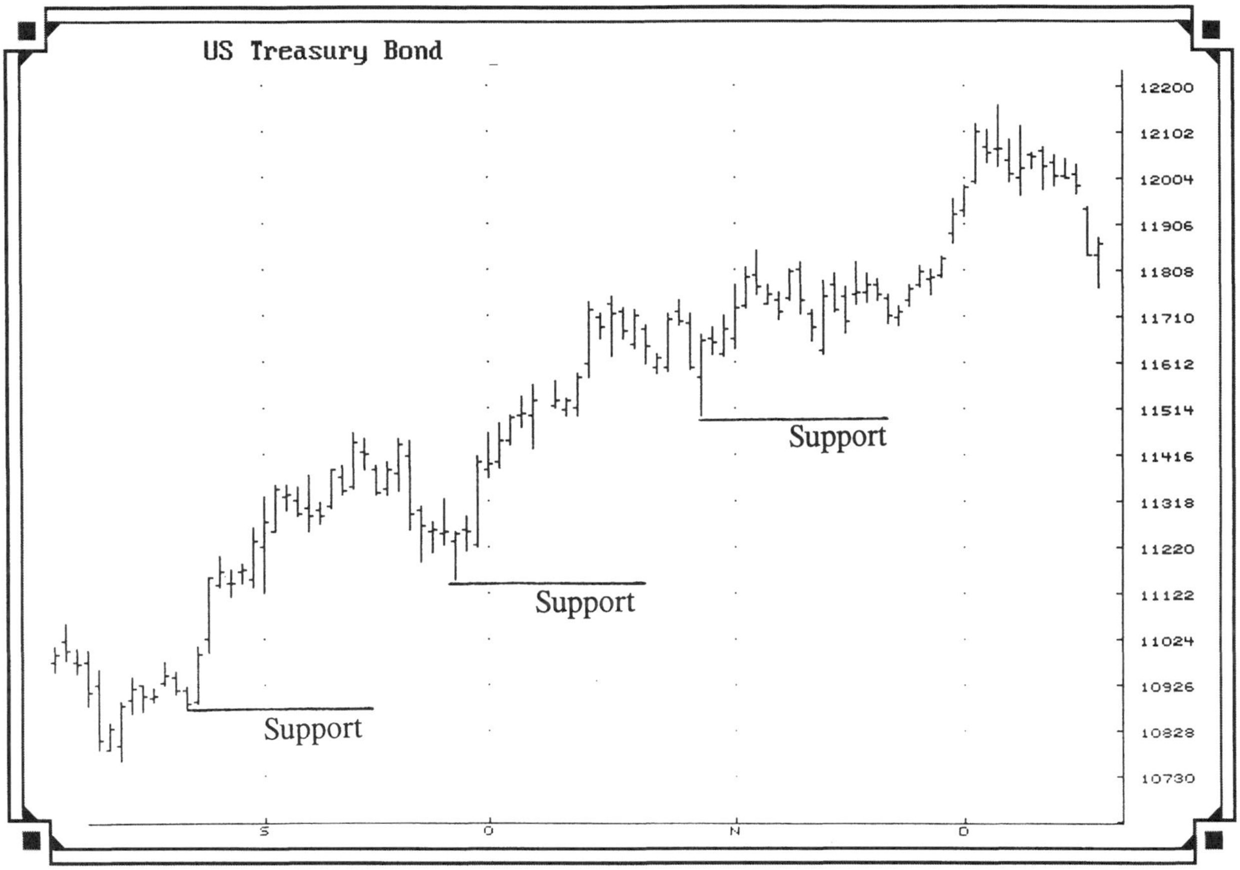

For a long position, place protective stops just under the support area. Should thc market continue to move up, place the protective stop up to the next level of support.

Support And Resistance
Example 3

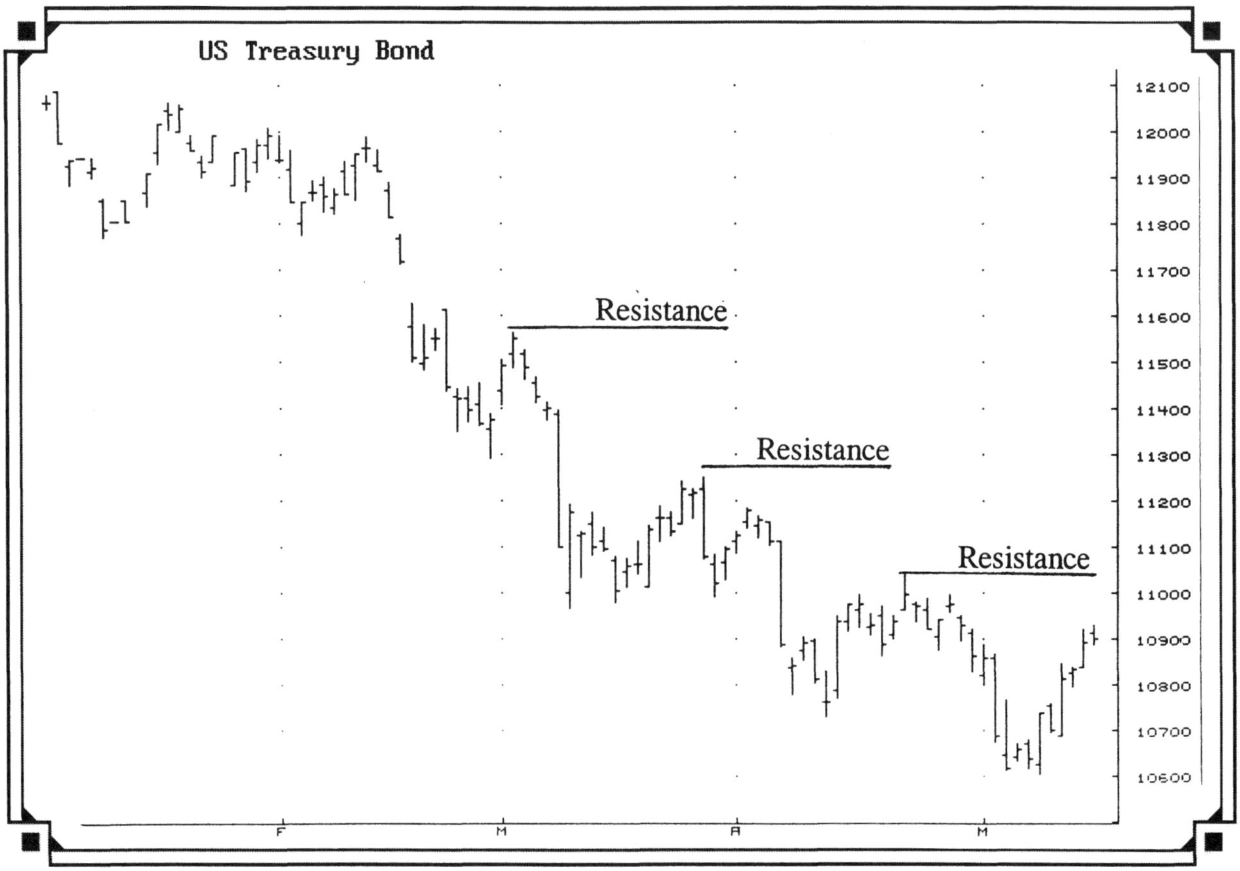

Sell the rallies at resistance levels and place protective stops above the upper channel line.

Chapter 5

THE SWINGING MARKET

Why does the market surge and then pullback? Is it a random action, or logical and numerically predictable? This chapter describes the patterns which typically dominate the swinging markets. The examples and summations given should logically demonstrate the theory behind market action and reaction.

What You Should Know About Reaction Swings

1. When the market rallies against its current trend one of three things happen:
    - The market is resting and will resume the trend within 3 to 7 days.
    - Something is causing a change and the market will correct itself with a new market trend.
    - A broken trendline is not expected when the market moves against the current trend. Therefore, investment is not likely.

2. As a general rule, market prices will retrace 3 to 7 days before continuing the trend.
    - Three to seven day retracements seem to help establish the areas of support and resistance found on your charts.
    - Generally, the price will come back to the support areas before moving higher.

3. In a down trending market, prices will retrace 3 to 7 days also, but they will come back to the resistance areas before moving lower again.
    - When the market rallies 3 to 7 days against the downward trend, it usually indicates a buy signal.

More About Reaction Swings

4. The Quick Flag occurs on a 2.5 day pullback.
   - This type of market action is a very strong trending market and will almost always come down to the lower channel line.
   - Should the movement against the trend be a normal retracement, enter a position only if the flag or pennant formation is broken in the direction of the trend.

5. If a flag formation in a down trending market exists, wait to take a position until the day the flag formation breaks in the direction of the trend.
   - In a very strong market, it may only rally up 2.5 to 3 days before falling again.

6. Place protective stops according to the market conditions
   - *Quick flag formation:* On a 2.5 day rally within a steep bearish channel place a protective stop just above the channel line of the rally.
   - *Bullish flag:* Place a protective stop just below the channel line of the pullback. Be ready to tighten up your protective stop after each pullback to the channel line.
   - *Bearish flag:* Place a protective stop just above the channel line of the rallies. Be ready to tighten up your protective stop after each rally to the channel line.

3 to 7 Day Retracement
Example 1

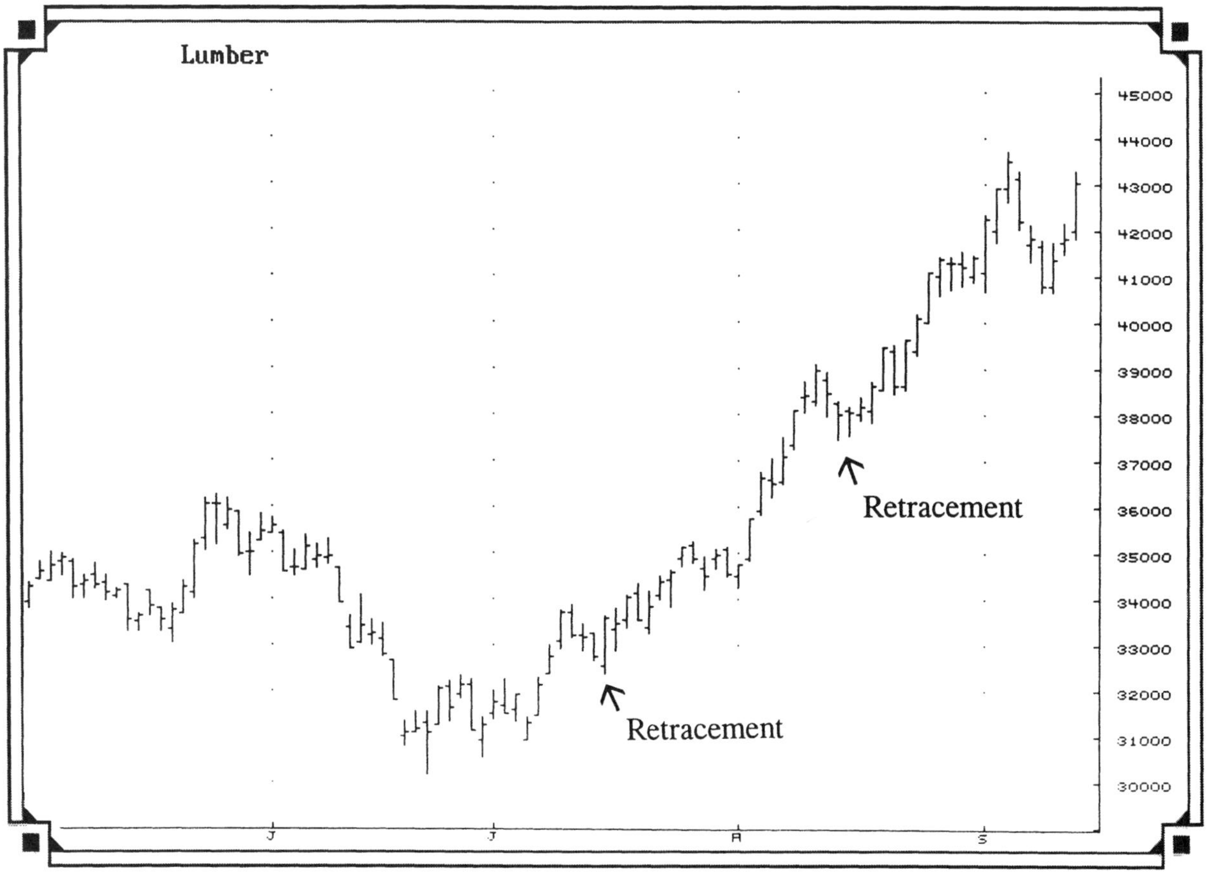

As the market moves up, it trends in a pattern of seven days up and three days down. The market will show strength in terms of the current market trend during a seven day upward movement. The three day pullback will occur when traders have been 'along for the ride' and decide to take some profits. Once they cash out their position, the market will 'pullback'. Few traders are willing to go short the market, therefore it usually reacts with low volume. In other words, the market is tired and needs a short nap.

"W" Formations
Example 1

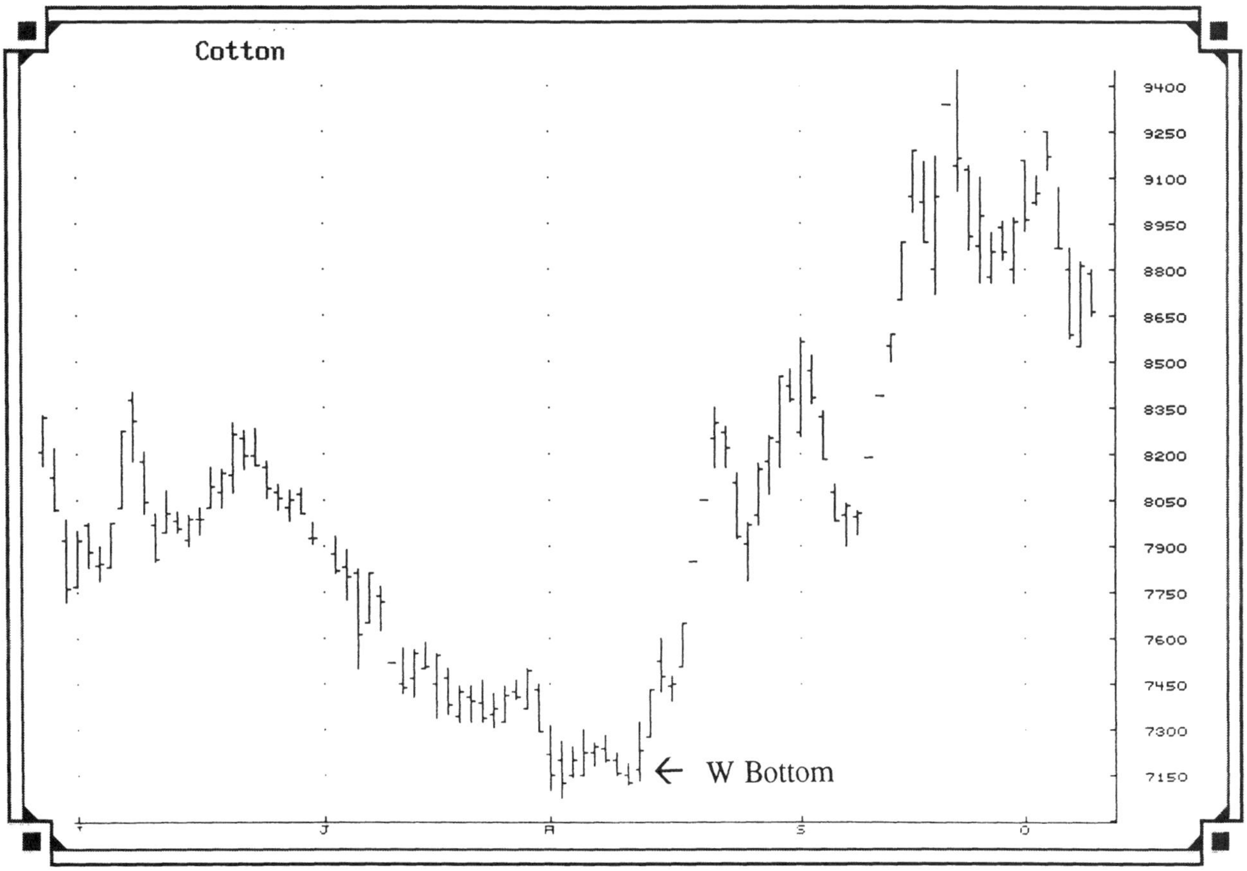

The 1-2-3 bottom (or the "W" bottom formation) normally consists of a 7 to 10 day pattern. It will then head higher once the downward trendline of the pullback breaks. This buy signal is usually very strong.

Strong Trending Market
Example 1

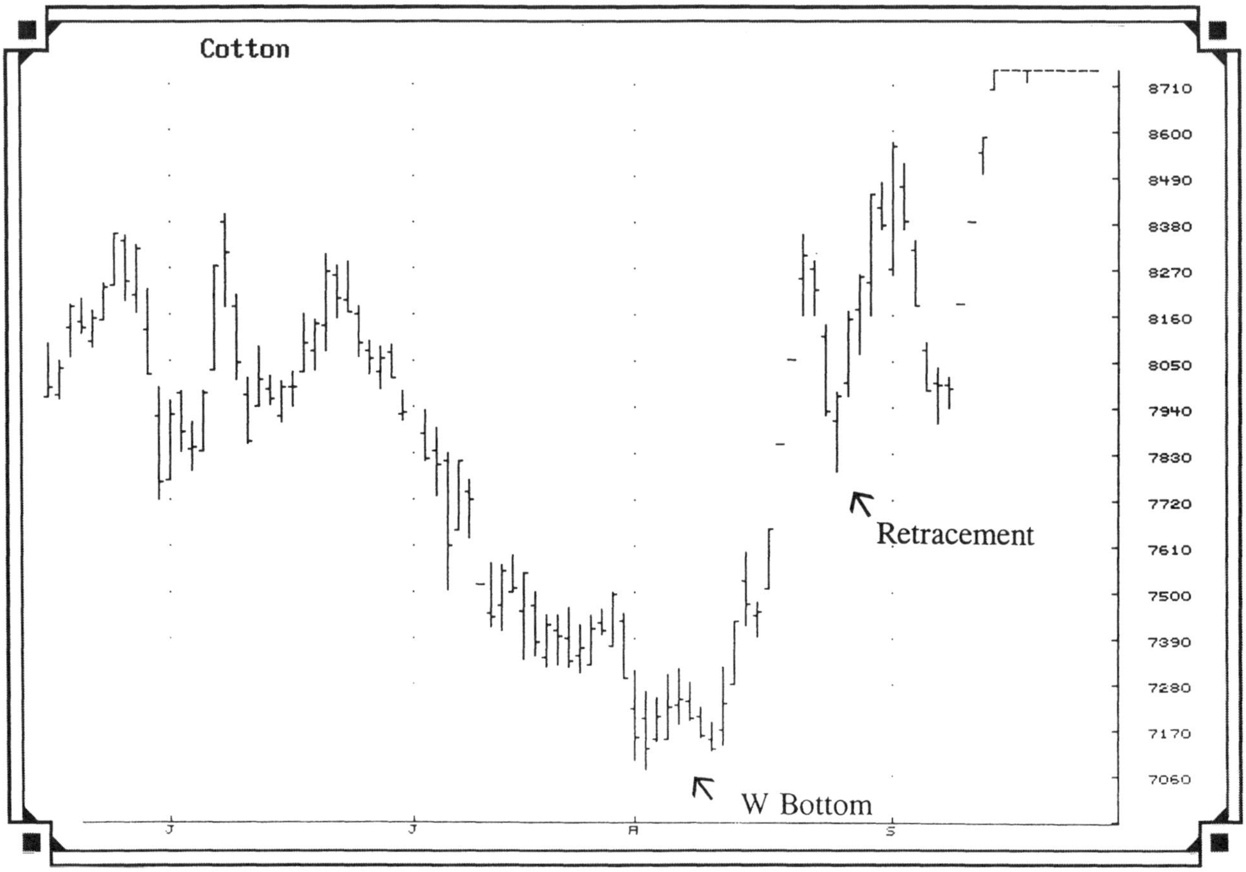

In a very strong bullish trend, the market may only pullback 2.5 to 3 days before running up again. It indicates a very strong trending market.

Three Day Retracements
Example 1

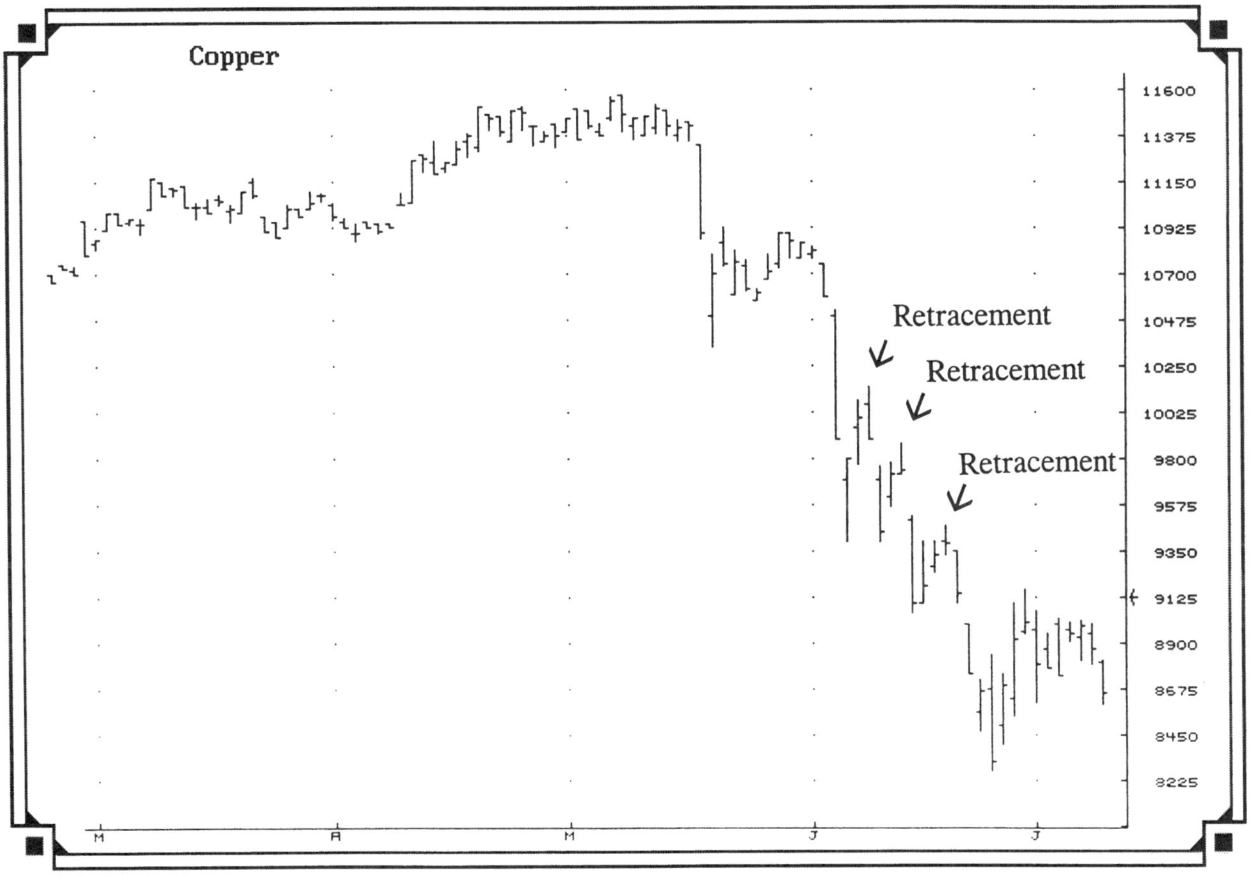

These two examples show how the 3 to 7 Day Retracement seem to establish the areas of support and resistance found on your charts. Retracements help put you in the market at a good price. In addition, retracements help determine where to place protective stops and when to move those stops upward.

Three Day Retracements
Example 2

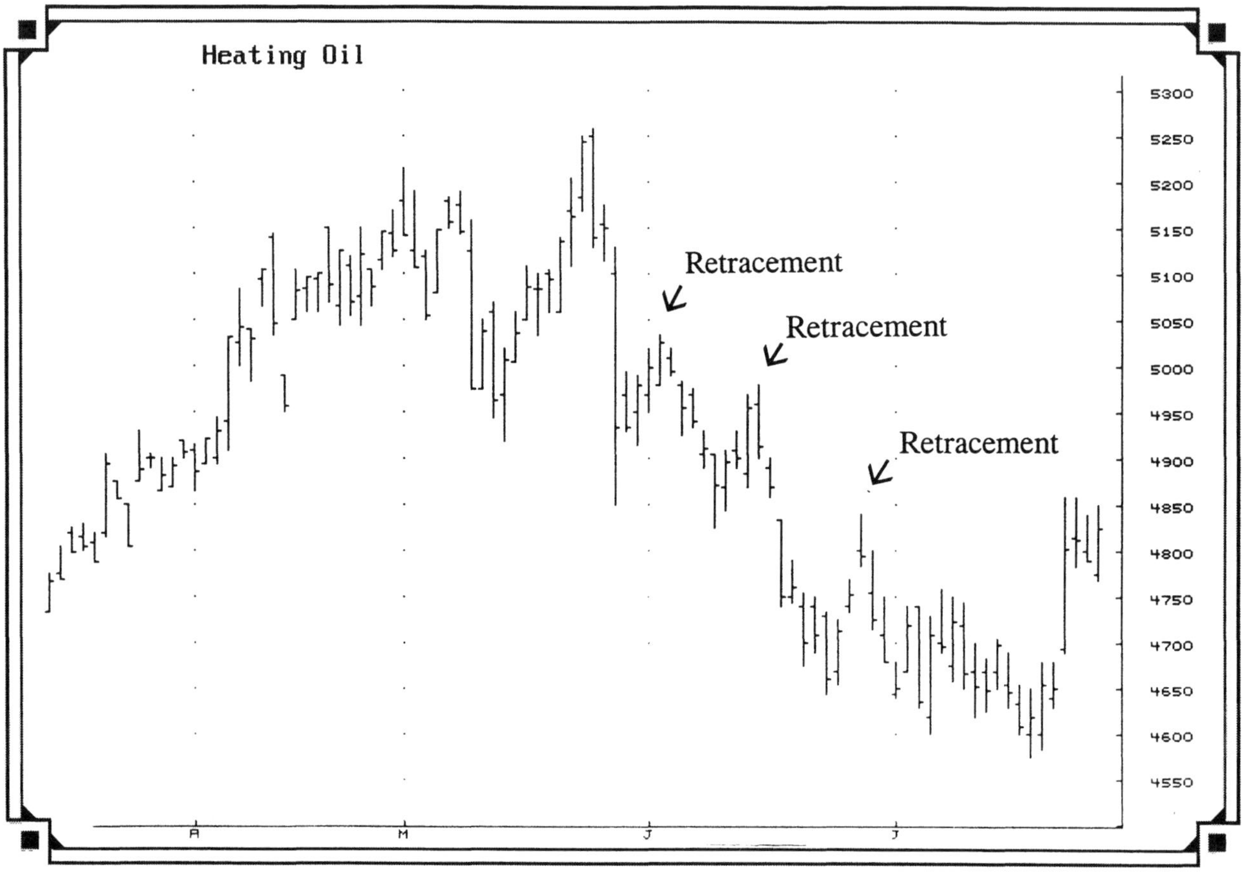

Trade this movement against the trend the same way. The sell signals come when the short term trendline (flag or pennant) breaks in the direction of the current trend.

Quick Flag
Example 1

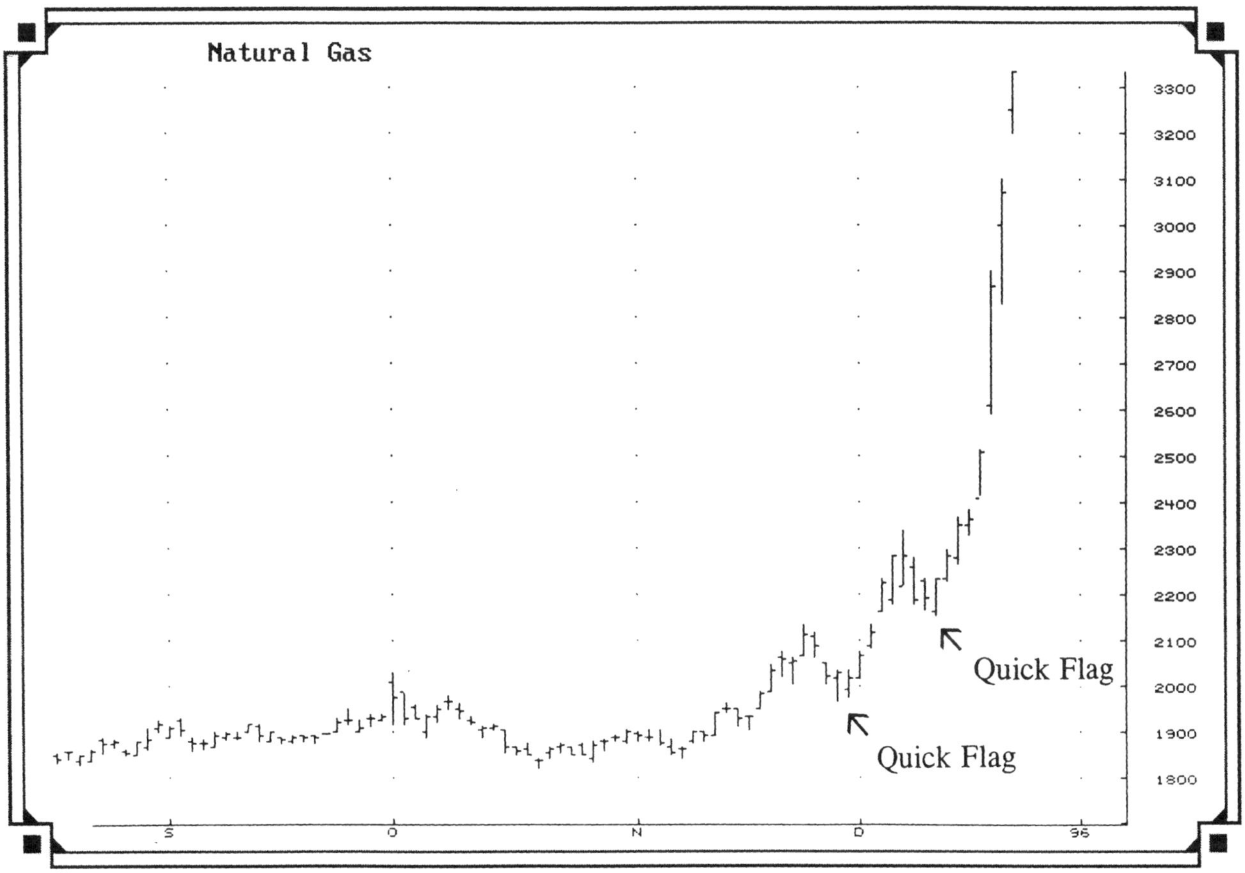

On this type of formation, (the quick flag on a 2.5 day pullback within a steep bullish channel), be aware the flag formation has broken to the upside. Place your protective stop just below the channel line of the pullback. In bearish markets, be prepared to sell once the flag formation breaks to the downside. Place a protective stop just above the channel line off of the highs. In either case, be ready to tighten up your protective stop after each pullback (or rally) to the channel line.

Chapter 6

THE REACTION CYCLE

How many times have you seen an amazing new product and said, "WOW! It's so simple why didn't I think of that?" That's how you will react once you see how the *Reversal Day Technique* works. First, we need to delve into what makes this technique perform with such flexibility...*the Reaction Swings.*

This chapter focuses on spotting the Reaction Swing. All it requires are two simple counting methods called the *reverse count* and the *forward count.* These tools makes our Reversal Day predictions uncomplicated, both in concept and execution.

Reaction Swings and Cycles

By now, you are aware that the market price will sometimes trade lower in a bull market (prices move higher) before it resumes an upward trend. There are also times in a bear market (prices move lower) when the market will trade higher for a short time before resuming the downward trend. These price pullbacks, called *reaction swings or retracements*, go against the trend. The beginning and end of the reaction swing are necessary to determine the center or the *reaction cycle*.

When searching for the reaction swing, it is permissible to go all the way to the beginning of the contract on an identified reaction swing. However, we recommend going back only *four or five weeks* because it allows for an easier identification of a new reaction. It also keeps the integrity of the Reversal Day projections strong. As you practice, look for a reaction swing that is followed by several market reversals. Try a reverse count and then a forward count (*see examples on pages 55-57)*. If your projected Reversal Days fall on the market reversals, you are on the correct reaction swing. If the projected days are off the market, go to the next reaction swing.

What You Should Know About Reaction Swings

1. Look for reaction swings (sometimes referred to as price pullbacks or retracements) that go against the trend.
   - A seven day *reaction swing* seems to work best, but adding days will still get accurate projections.
   - An identified reaction cycle can continue all the way to the beginning of that contract. However, it is best to *only go back four to five weeks.*
   - A reaction swing formation *must have a minimum of three days* from the high close to the low close.

2. The center of the reaction cycle is determined by the beginning and the end of reaction swings.

3. When looking for the high of the reaction swing, find the day with the highest closing price.

4. The low of the reaction swing will be on the day with the lowest closing price.

The next two examples show reaction swings from two different markets. The bull market example illustrates prices moving higher. The bear market example (on the following page) shows the prices moving lower.

Reaction Swing--Bull Market
Example 1

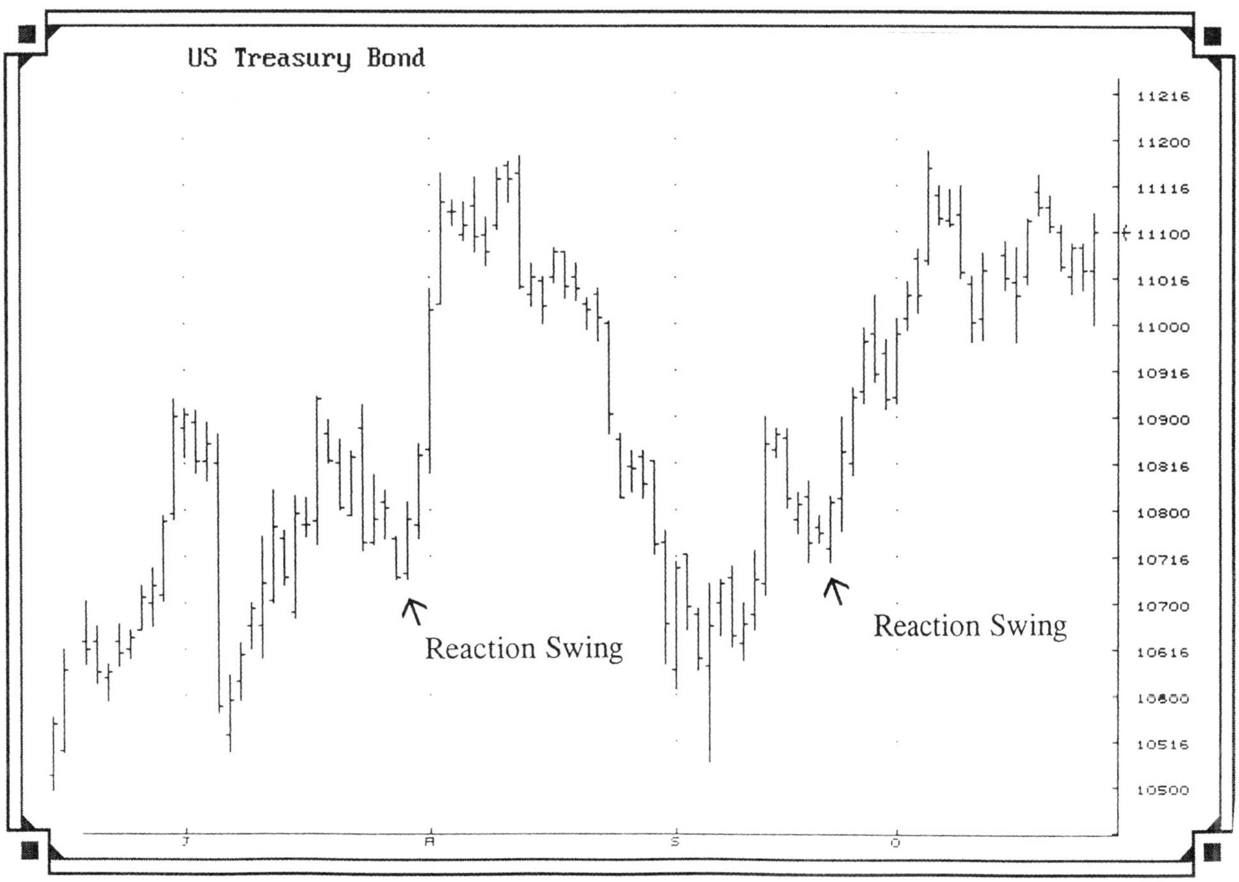

Reaction Swing--Bear Market
Example 2

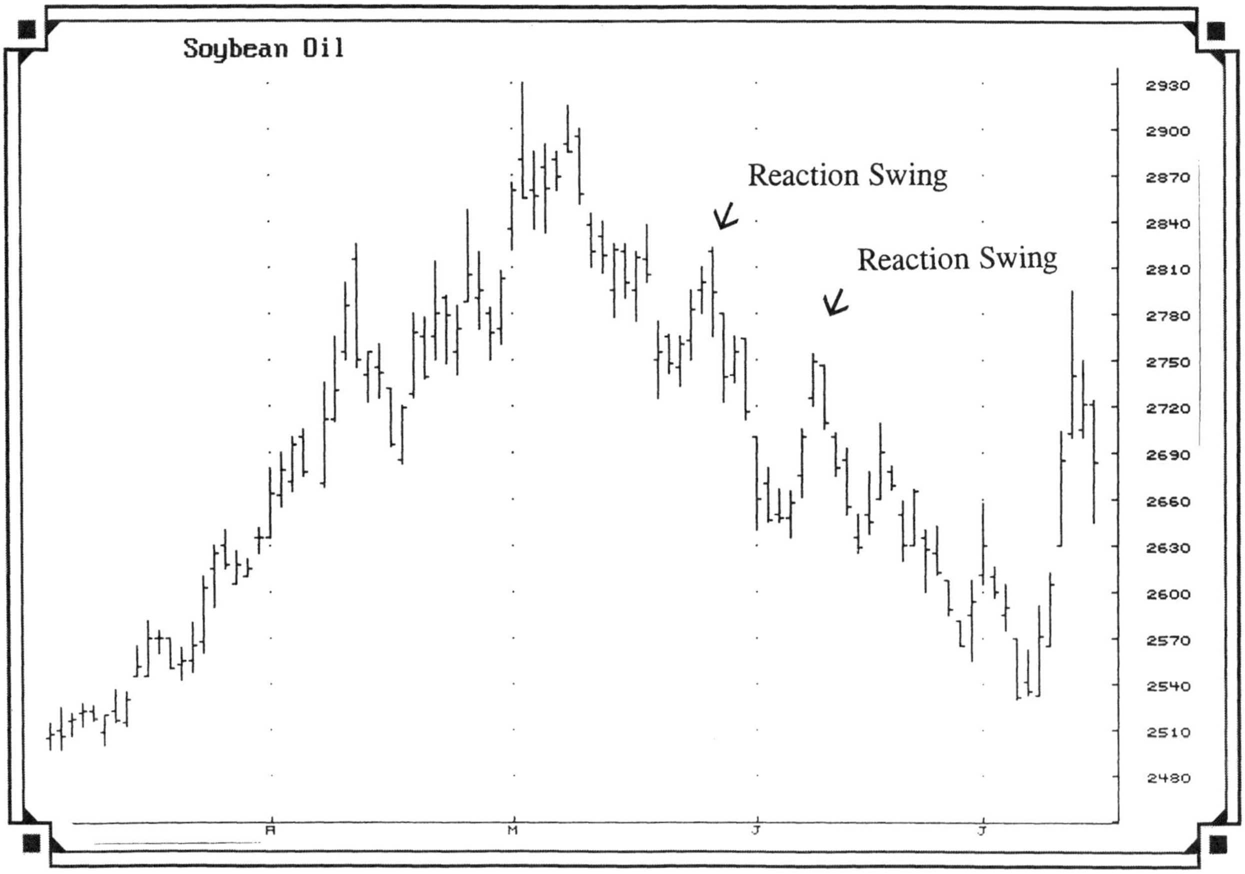

Reaction Swing
Example 3

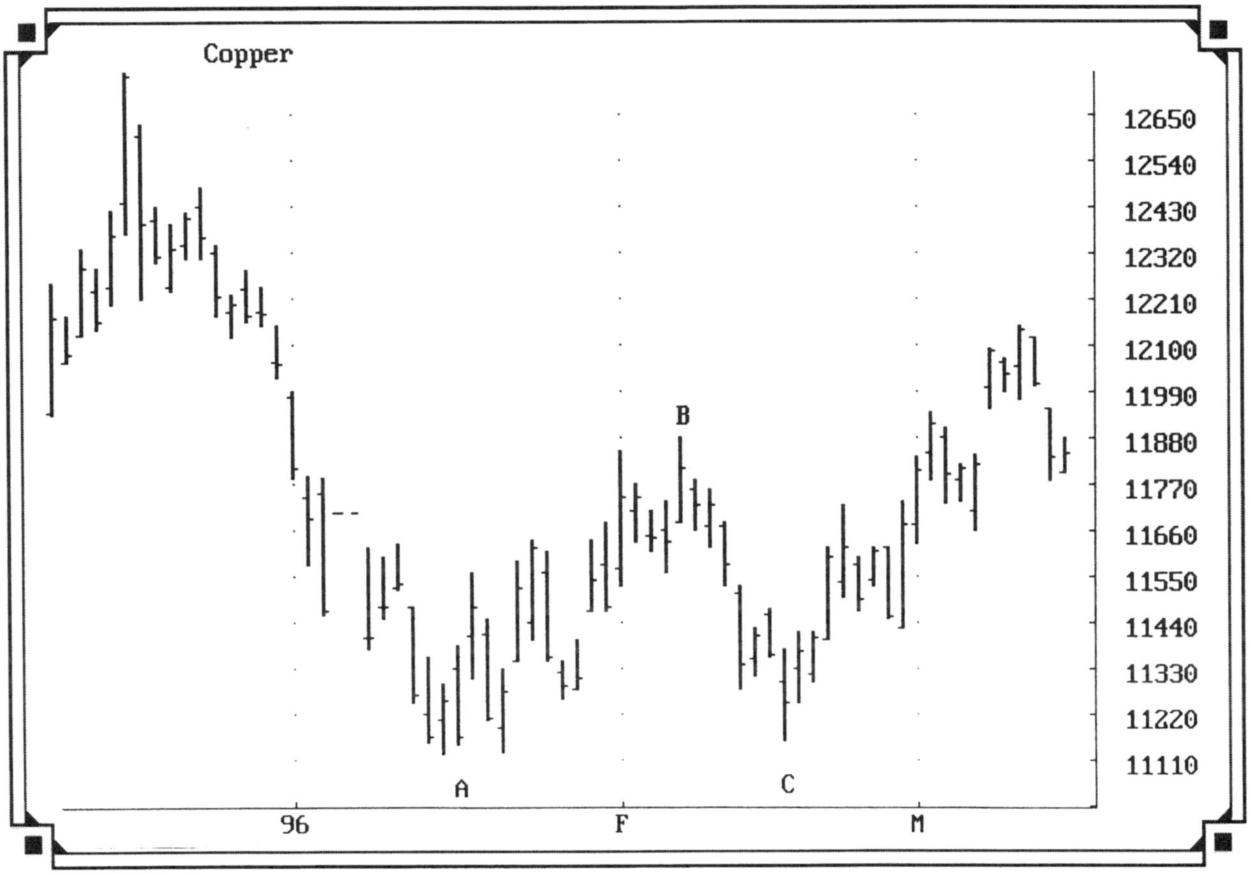

In this example, the market makes a low (A) then establishes a high (B). From this high, the market trades lower for a short time until it hits a low (C). At this point, it resumes the original trend.

The move from (A) to (B) represents the *trend of the market*, and the move from (B) to (C) is the reaction swing *against this trend*. Once the reaction swings completes its cycle, the market resumes the original trend.

Chapter 7

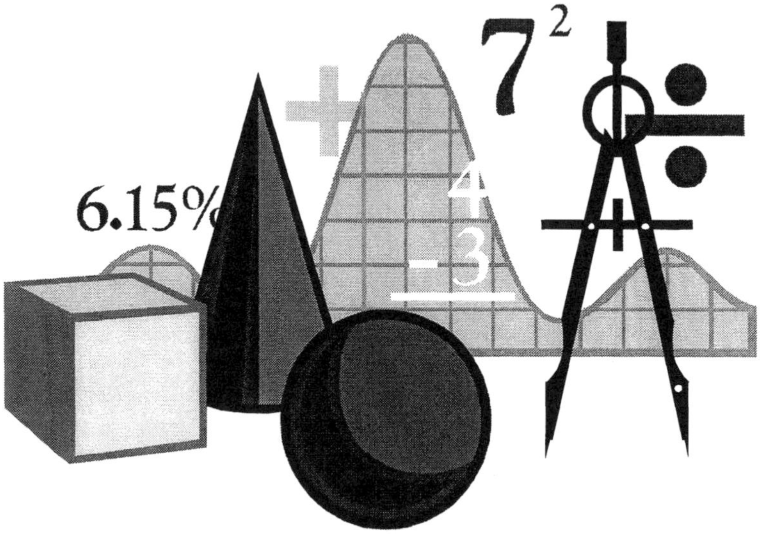

LEARNING TO COUNT

Now that you know how to identify the reaction swing, projecting the Reversal Day will be easy.

In this chapter you will learn how to combine the Reaction Swing with the reverse and forward counting method.

Reverse Count

Once you find the Reaction Swing, all you need to do is apply a *reverse count and forward count.* You start with the reverse count. This starts from the beginning of the Reaction Swing. It is important to remember, in a market that is trending *downward, the beginning of the Reaction Swing is the lowest closing price* before the market trades higher against the current trend. In a market that is trending *upward, the beginning of the Reaction Swing is the highest close* before the market trades lower against the current trend.

In a market trending lower the reverse count will always count back to the *lows.* Therefore, in a market trending higher, the reverse count will always count back to the *highs.*

What You Should Know About Reverse Counts

1. Reverse Count in a downward trending market:
   - Mark the low of the Reaction Swing.
   - The Reaction Swing low is the *lowest closing day* before the market trades higher against the current trend.
   - The Reverse Count always starts on the day before the beginning of the Reaction Swing. (On the charts, this is the day to the *left of the lowest closing price* of the reaction swing.)

2. Reverse Count in an upward trending market:
   - Mark the high of the Reaction Swing.
   - The Reaction Swing high is the *highest closing day* before the market trades lower against the current trend.
   - The Reverse Count always starts on the day before the beginning of the Reaction Swing. (On the charts, this is the day to the *left of the highest closing price* of the Reaction Swing.)

3. Once the market forms a new Reaction Swing you can start a new Reverse Count.

4. Remember to count holidays in your calculations, even if the markets are closed.

Reverse Count
Example 1

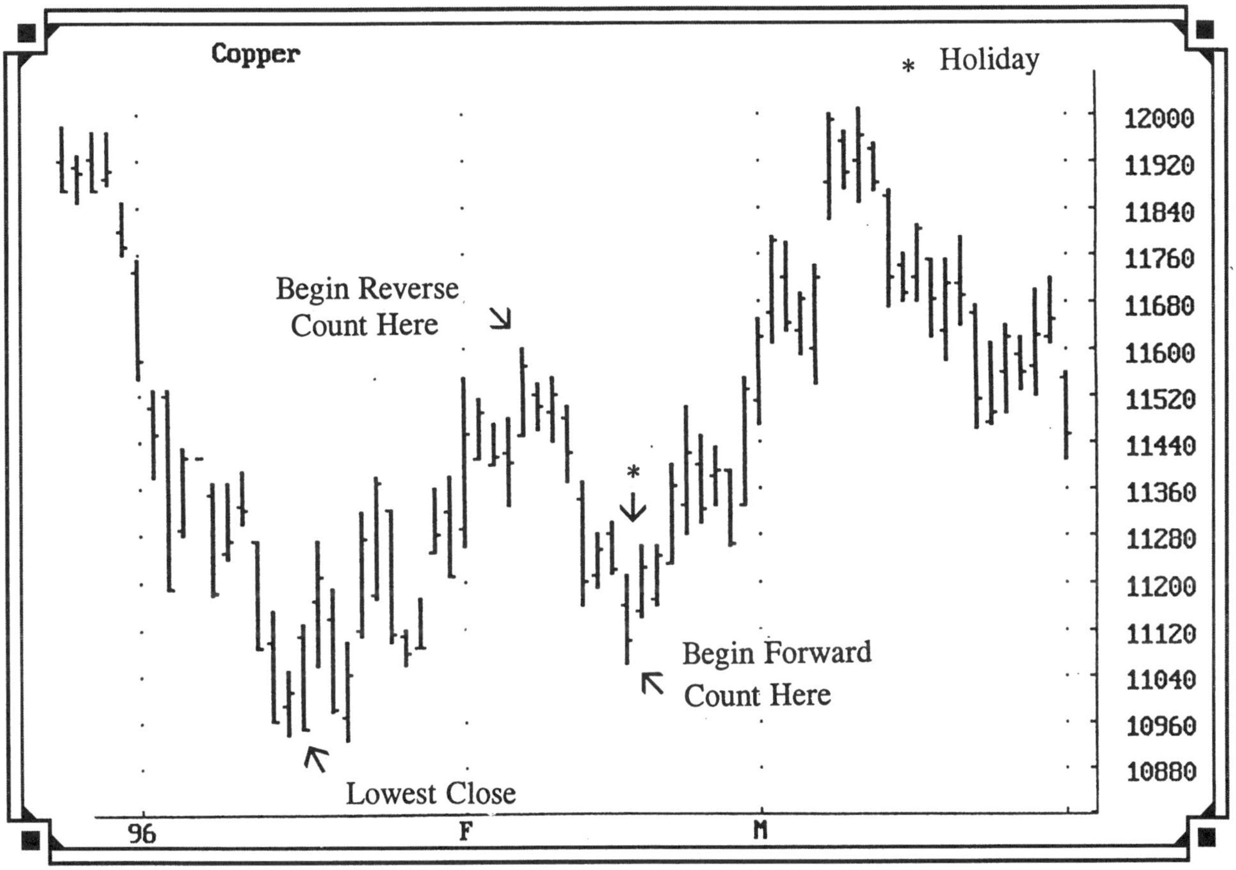

Copper made a bottom in mid January and is now trading in an upward trend. A Reaction Swing formed in February offering a point to begin a *new reverse count.* Starting from *the highest close of the Reaction Swing count back to the last low close* (Marked on the chart above). Remember, as described on page 60, *when counting back to a downward trending market, count to the lowest close of the swing patterns.* In this case the lowest close was also the end on the downward trend.

Reverse Count
Example 2

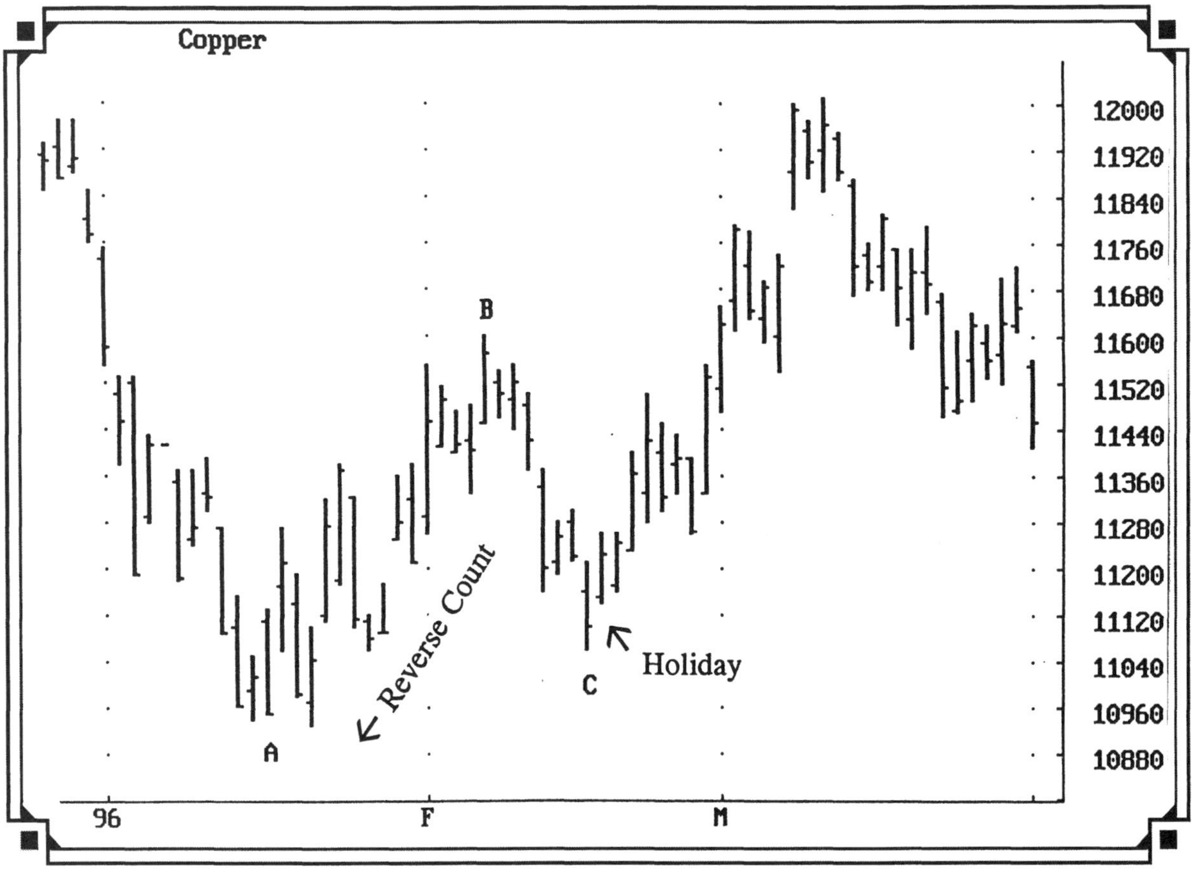

This Copper chart demonstrates a reverse count. The market had posted a low (A), then traded higher, making an intermediate high (B). The market then trades lower into (C), before resuming the original trend. Once the market trades above the high (B) the Reaction Swing is complete. Now apply the reverse count. Starting on the day before the Reaction Swing high (the first day to the left on the chart) count backwards to the lowest close (A) which marks the end of a downward trend.

Reverse Count

Example 3

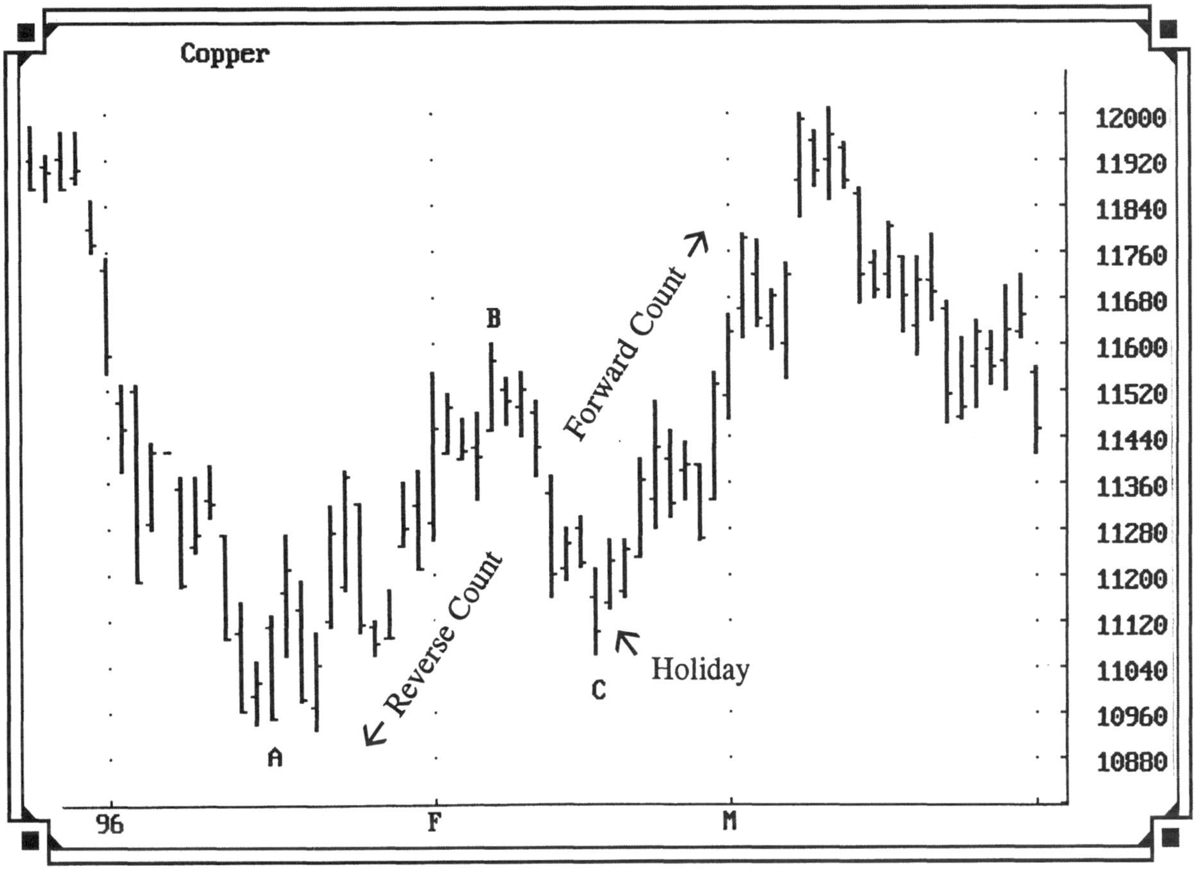

Now apply the forward count. From the lowest close of the Reaction Swing (C) count forward (starting with the first day to the right of the lowest close). Count forward the equal amount of days calculated during the reverse count, in this example it is 15 days. You will end just one day after the highest close of this strong upward move. Now refer to (C) on thc Copper chart. The lowest close occurred on a Friday. The following Monday was President's Day and all the market were closed. However, include this extra day in your forward count. You should finish the forward count on the day with the *highest closing price before the market reverses and begins a major downward trend.*

Reverse Count Relates To Forward Count
Example 1

This chart demonstrates how to project new Reversal Days by using the newest reaction swing.

To better illustrate the relationship between the reverse count and the forward count, this example measures from the exact center of the reaction swing. In other words, the reverse count identifies the future turning point in the markets.

Mark the reaction swing on this Coffee chart (B) and (C). Note that the market is in a downward trend. Therefore, in the reverse count, mark only the lowest close of the previous reaction swings. Count backward from the day before the low (B). The lowest closing price of the previous reaction swing (A) falls on the ninth day. Remember, count the Labor Day holiday. Count forward nine days which is the day with lowest closing price (D).

This day began a five day rally.

Reverse Count Relates To Forward Count

Example 1

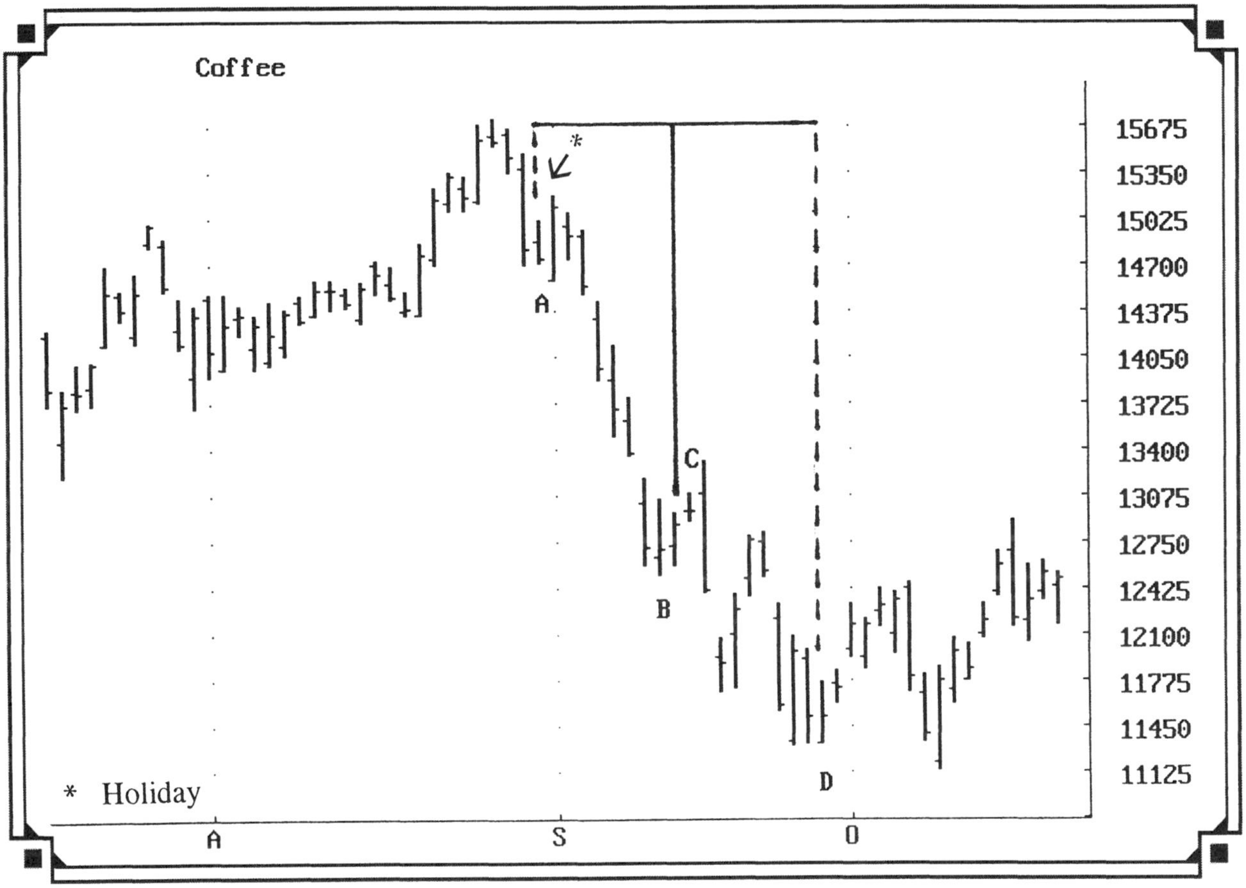

More Reverse Moves

Example 2

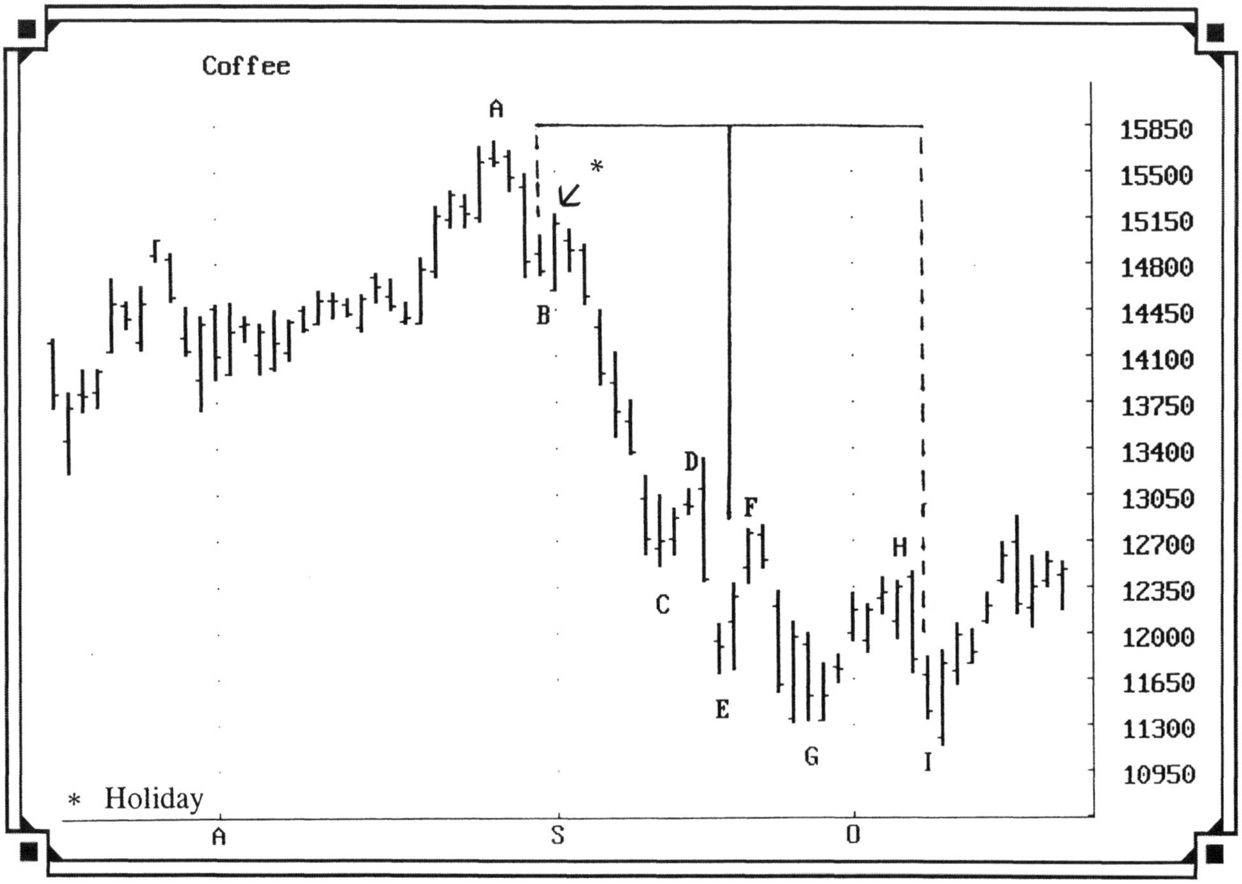

Now it is time to take the reverse count a little further. This is the same Coffee chart used in the previous example. The market formed a new reaction swing marked (E) and (F). Counting backward from the low (E) to the previous lows marked by (C) and (B), you should end up with a count of 4 and 13. Now, counting forward the same number of days, you will find that the fourth day just happens to be a low (G) before a six day rally. The 13th day (I) marks the major low of the downward trend.

Timing Reverse Moves
Example 3

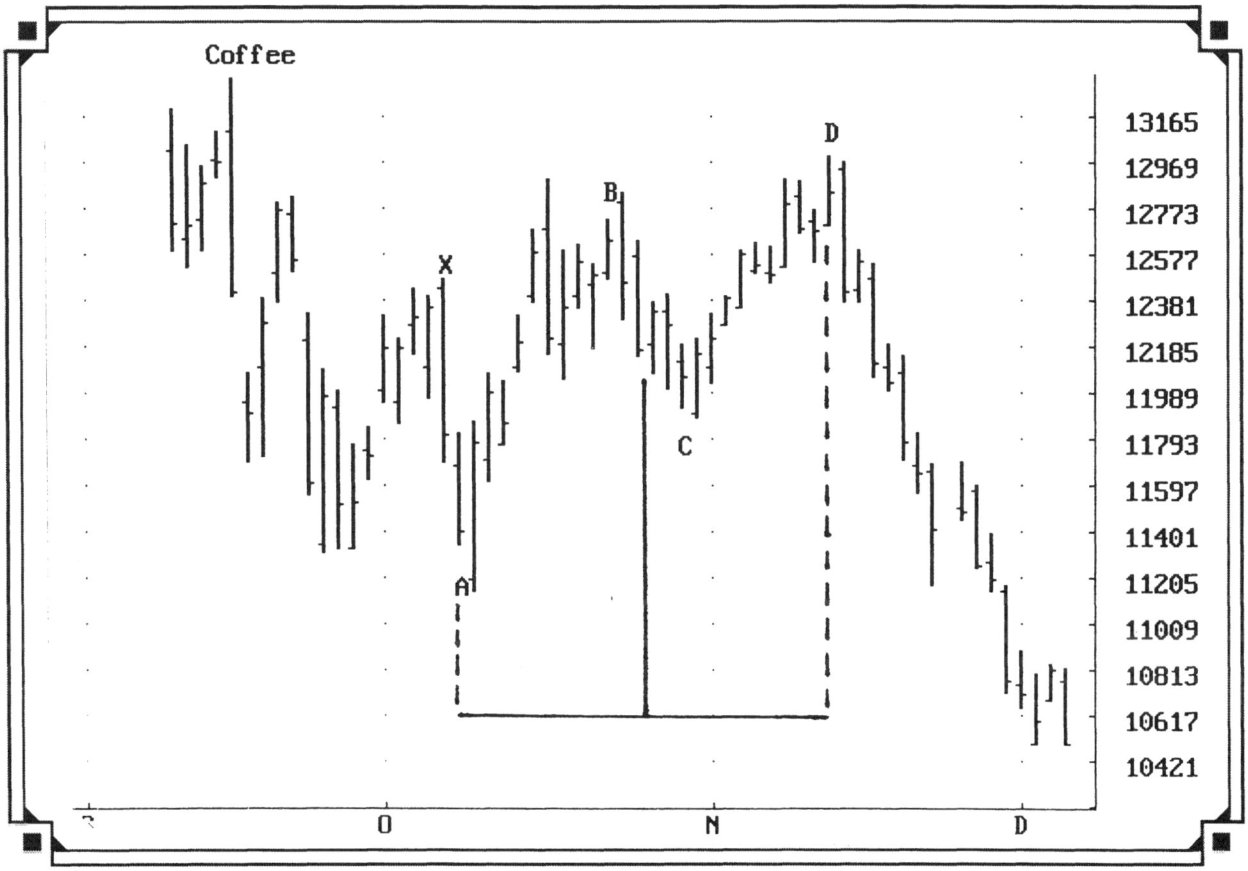

The reaction swing on this chart is marked as (B) and (C). Now count backward to (A). This marks the low in the downward trend. The reverse count calculation equals 10 days to the lowest close. Now count forward from the lowest close of the reaction swing (B)/(C). Counting forward 10 days identifies (D) as the projected Reversal Day. This Reversal Day was not only the highest price, but also the highest closing price of the rally. A sharp 16 day fall in the Coffee market followed.

Chapter 8

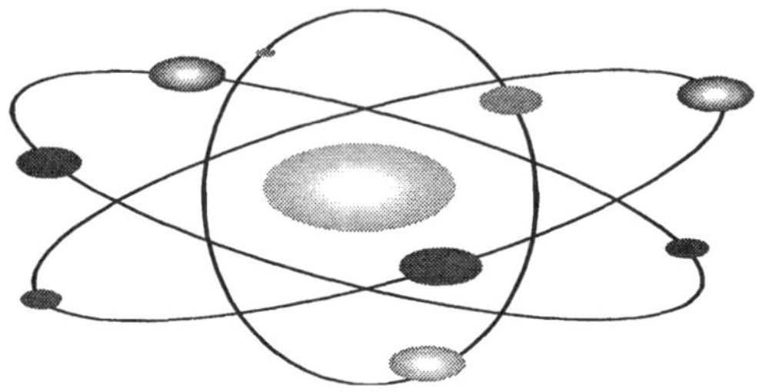

CONTINUING THE REACTION CYCLE

The futures market is very fluid and changes constantly. That is why many analytical methods that work with bull markets will not work in bear markets. Similarly, methods that predict trending markets will not function in a consolidating market. The greatest challenge for any trader is to find an approach which works well in *any market condition.*

We've said it before, but it's worth repeating. The Reversal Day Technique is flexible enough to meet this challenge because it combines three essential ingredients: time, price and confirming patterns. This chapter takes a look at one of those magic ingredients...TIME!

Reaction Cycle
Example 1

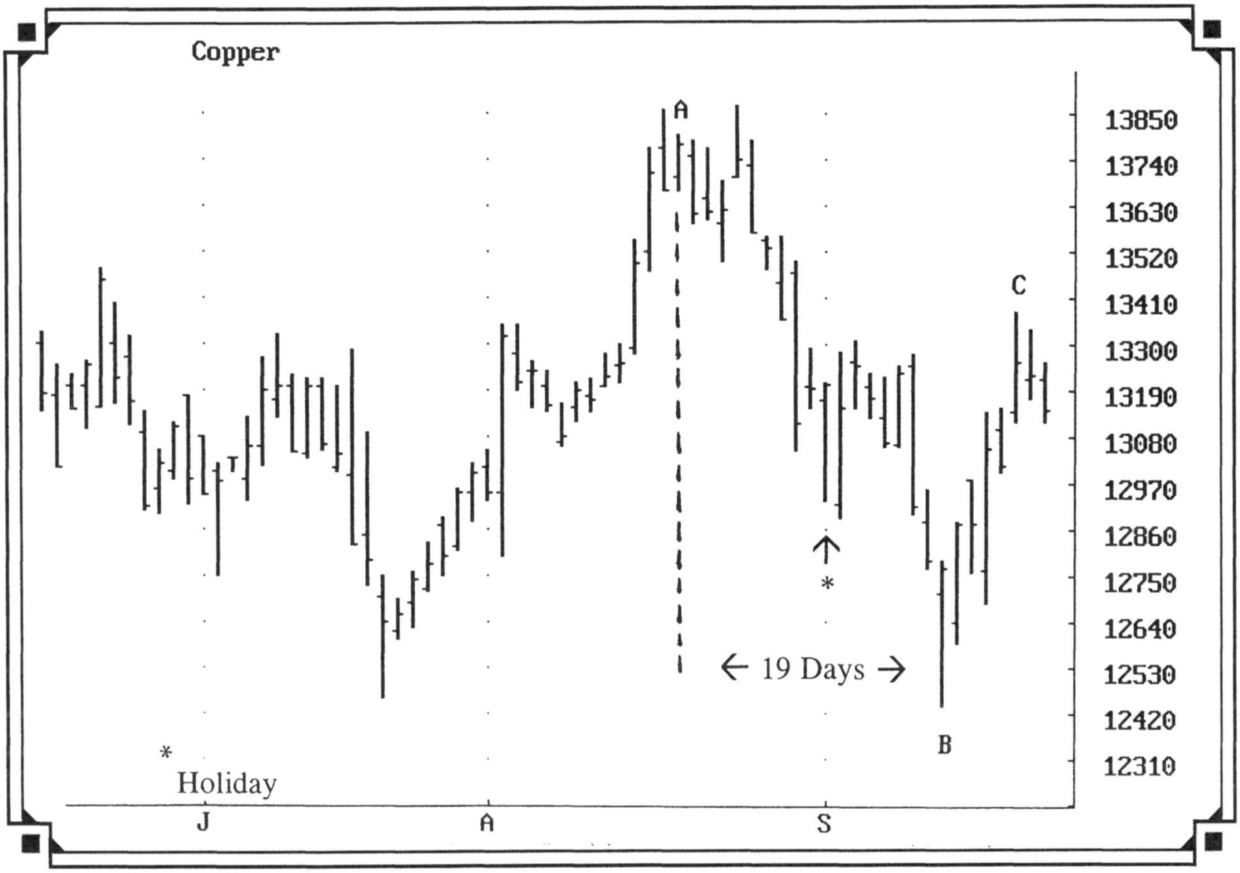

Back in early October, few people realized that a pattern just formed on the December Copper chart. This pattern identified three major turning points that occurred in Copper over the next three months. The identified reaction swing is marked as (B) and (C) on the above chart. We spot the lowest close of the reaction swing marked (B) and begin our reverse count until we hit the highest close of the upward trend. Then, count 19 days. Add one day because of the Labor Day holiday and perform the forward count. If you counted forward 19 days the projected Reversal Day landed on October 19.

Reaction Cycle
Example 2

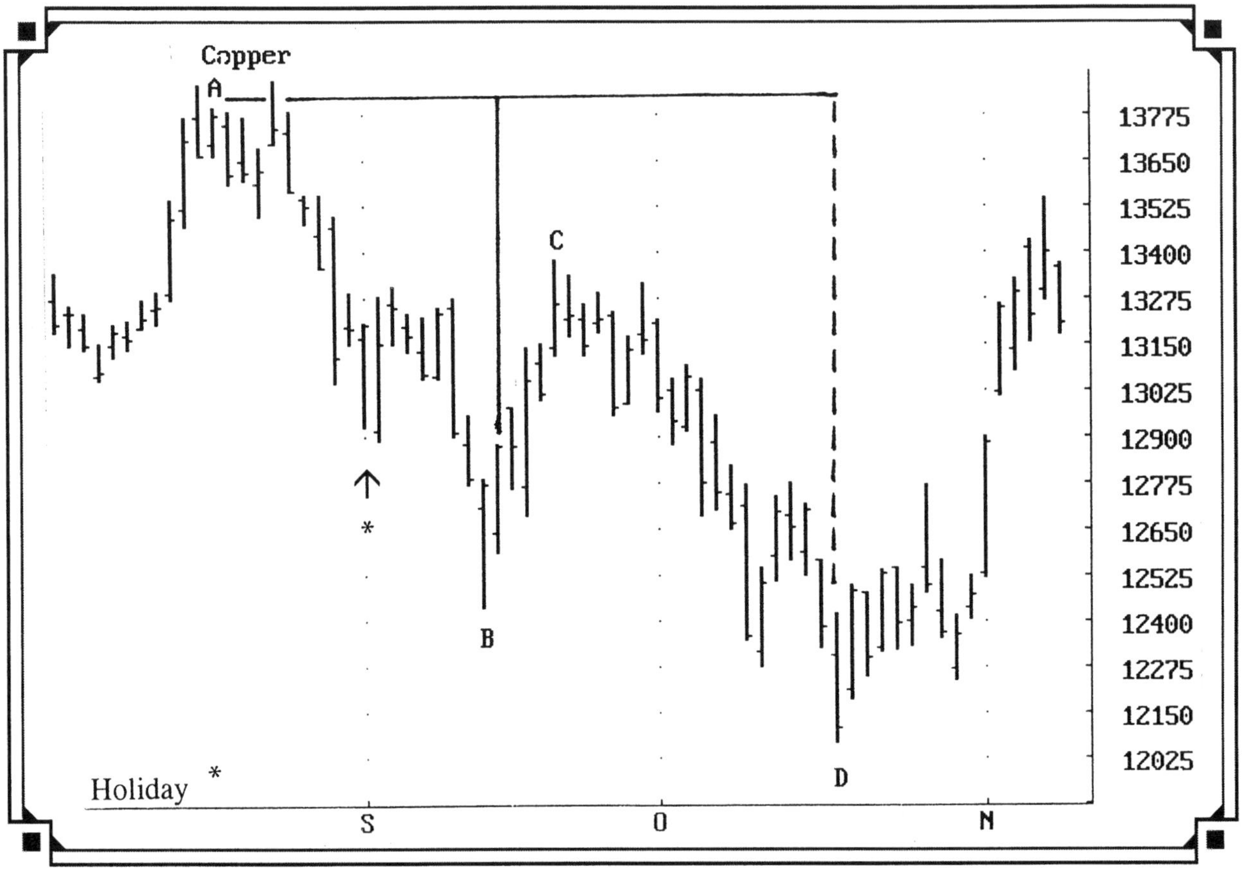

The Copper high of this reaction swing occurred on Sept. 12. From there it continued its downward trend for 19 days. It posted a low on October 19 (D). This day proved to be the lowest closing price on a major downward move for Copper.

Reaction Cycle
Example 3

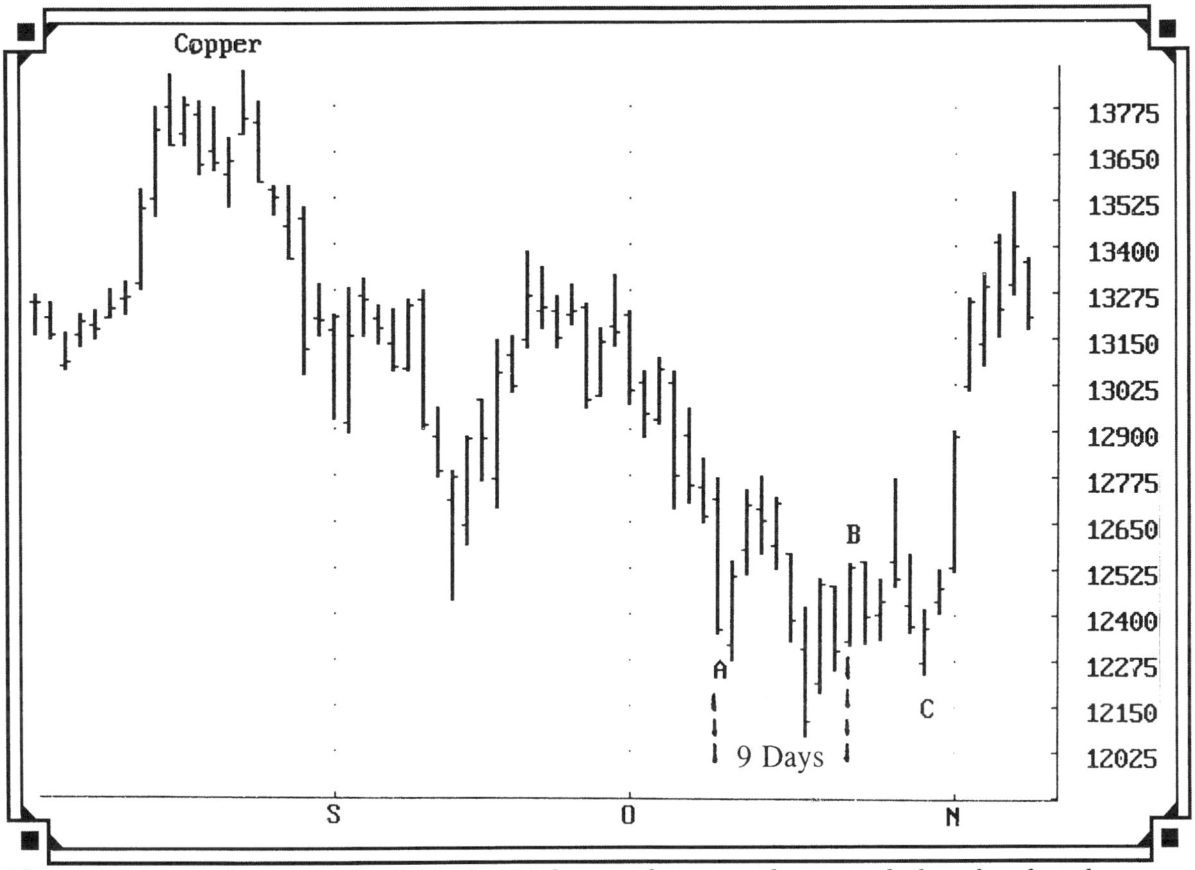

Note: In this example, we used the closing low (A) because the contract low was only three days from the reaction swing. We recommend at least five days after the reaction swing (though fewer days may sometimes work.).

From the contract low the market traded higher and formed a new reaction swing marked (B) (C) on the chart. It is now time to do a reverse count from this reaction swing. From the highest close (B) start counting backwards, *starting on the day before* (B). Count back to the lowest close (A)**. The reverse count is nine days. Now count forward nine days from (C*), starting on the day following* (C). This projects the next Reversal Day to be November 10.

Reaction Cycle
Example 4

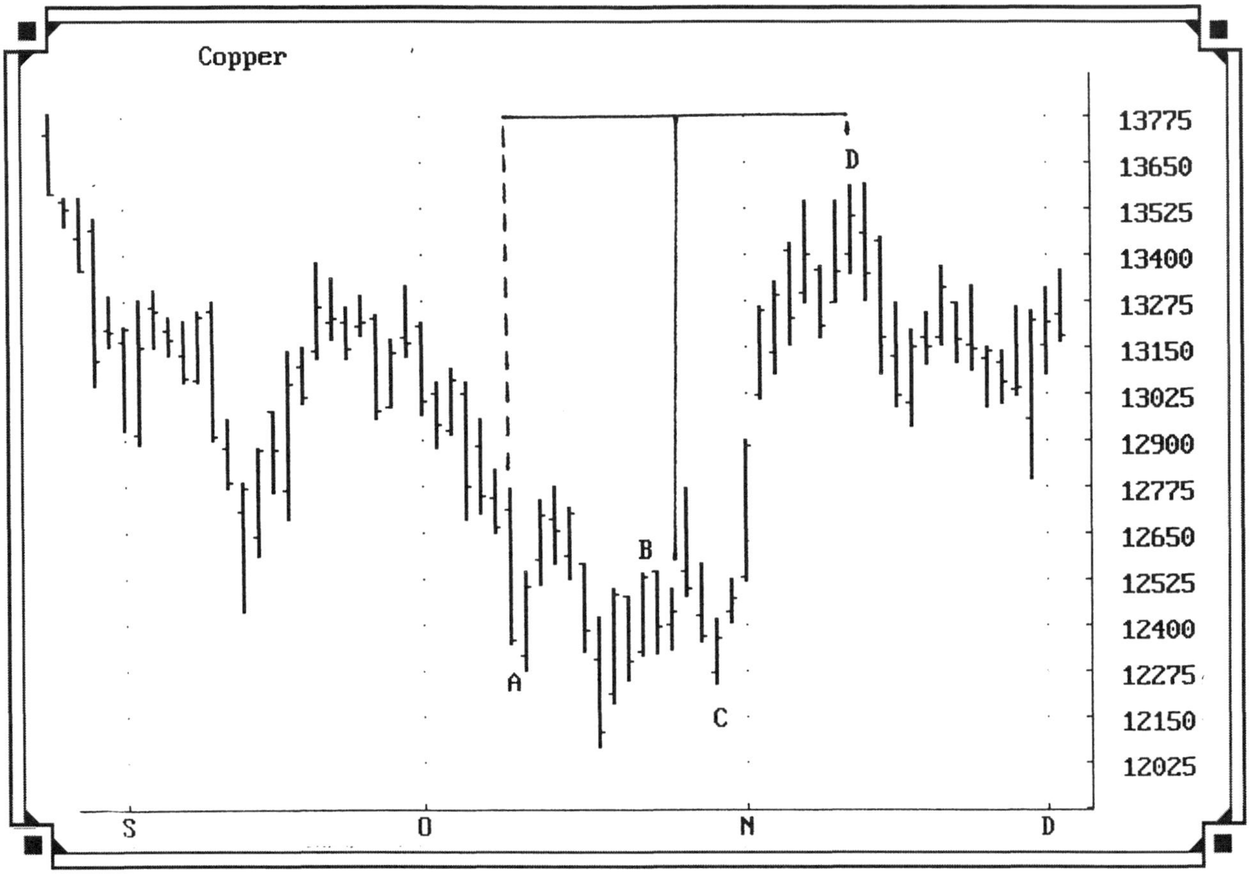

Copper traded sharply higher for 9 days from the low of the reaction swing (B) and (C). As projected, the highest closing price of the move landed on November 10th.

Reaction Cycle
Example 5

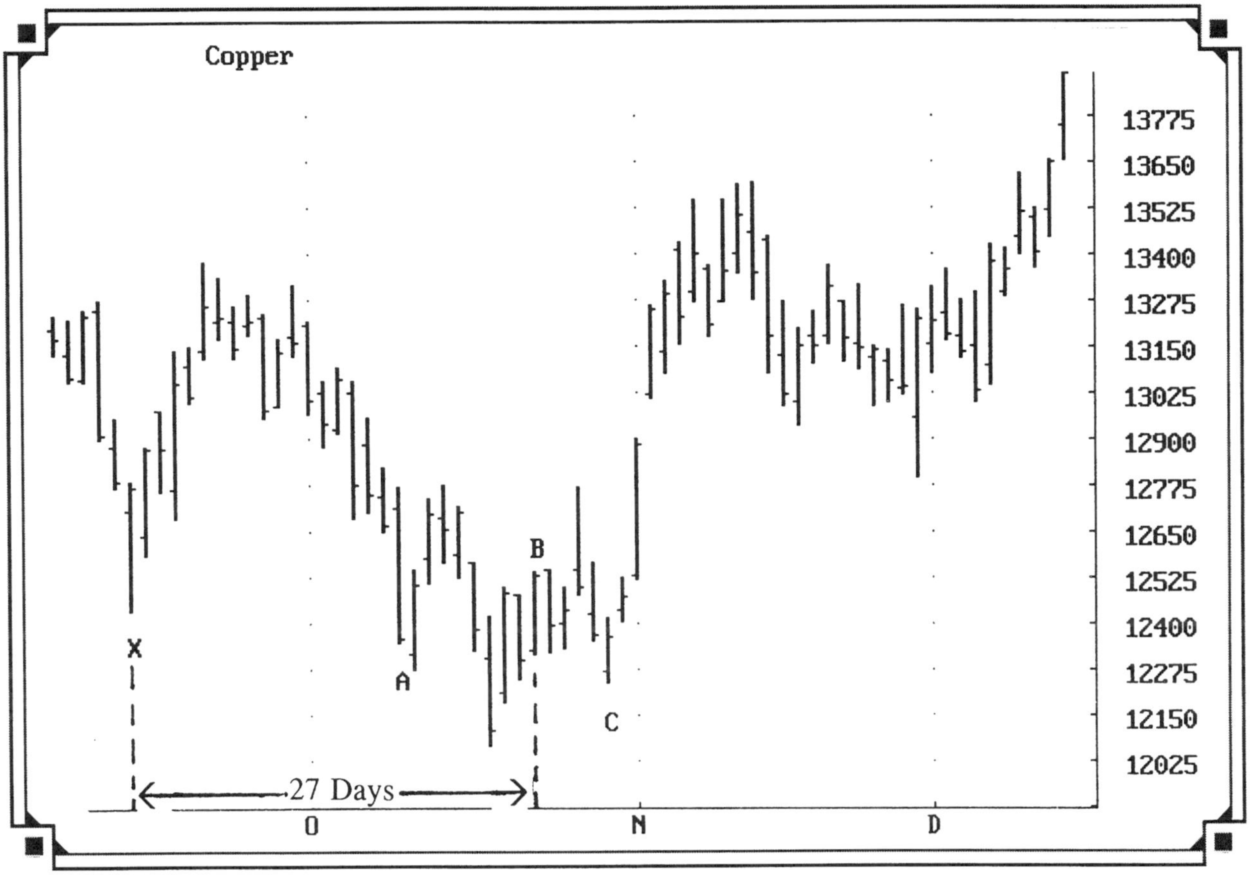

Let's take the reverse count a little further than the previous example. Go to the lowest close of the original reaction swing. The reverse count from the reaction swing, ((B) and (C)), to this low close (X) should be 27 days.

The forward count from the low of the reaction swing (B) and (C) suggests December 6 will be the next Reversal Day.

Reaction Cycle
Example 6

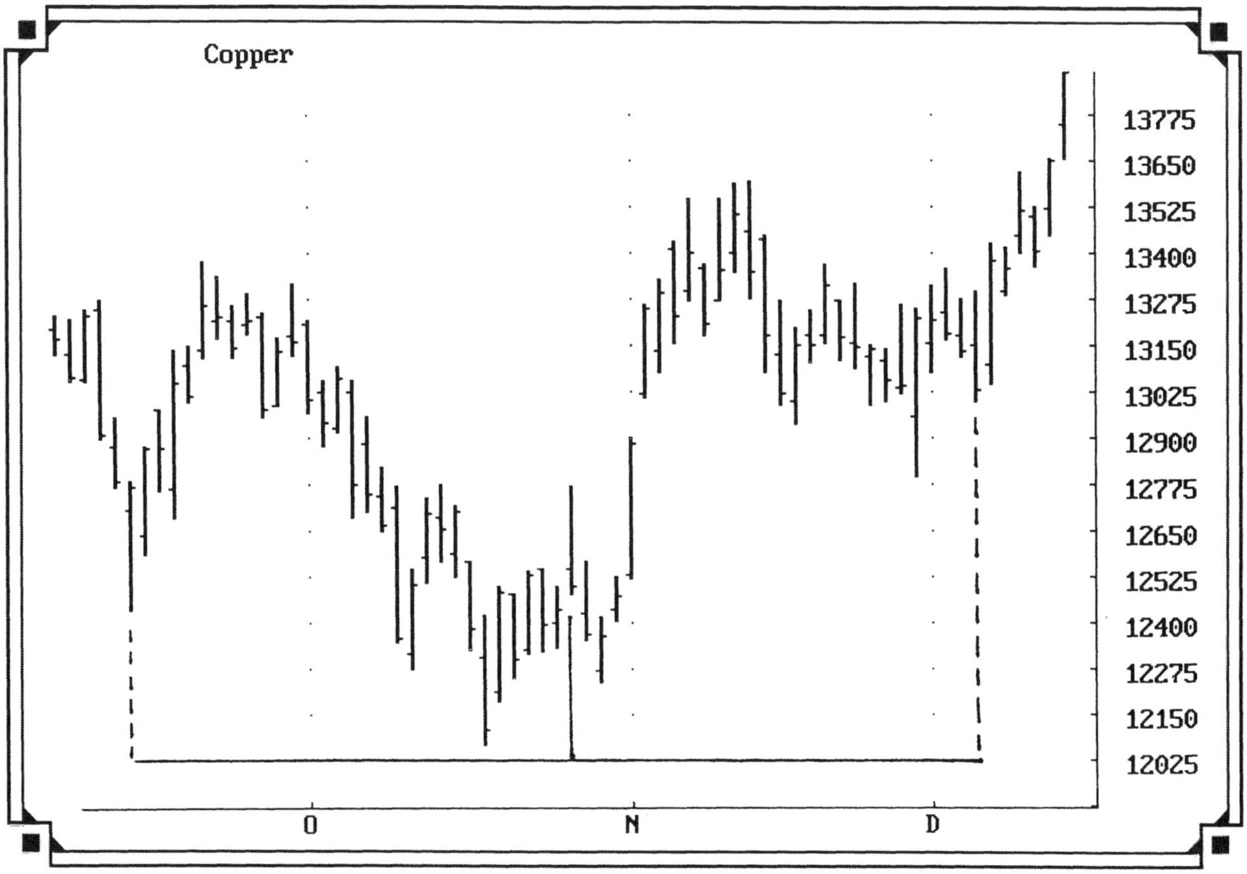

In this chart, Copper traded sideways to lower for the next couple of weeks. Remember, even though the Copper market closed for two days due to the Thanksgiving Holiday, we still count these two days as trading days.

After this consolidation time, the market began a strong rally. However, this did not occur until it established the lowest closing price of the correction phase on the predicted date of December 6.

Reaction Cycle
Example 7

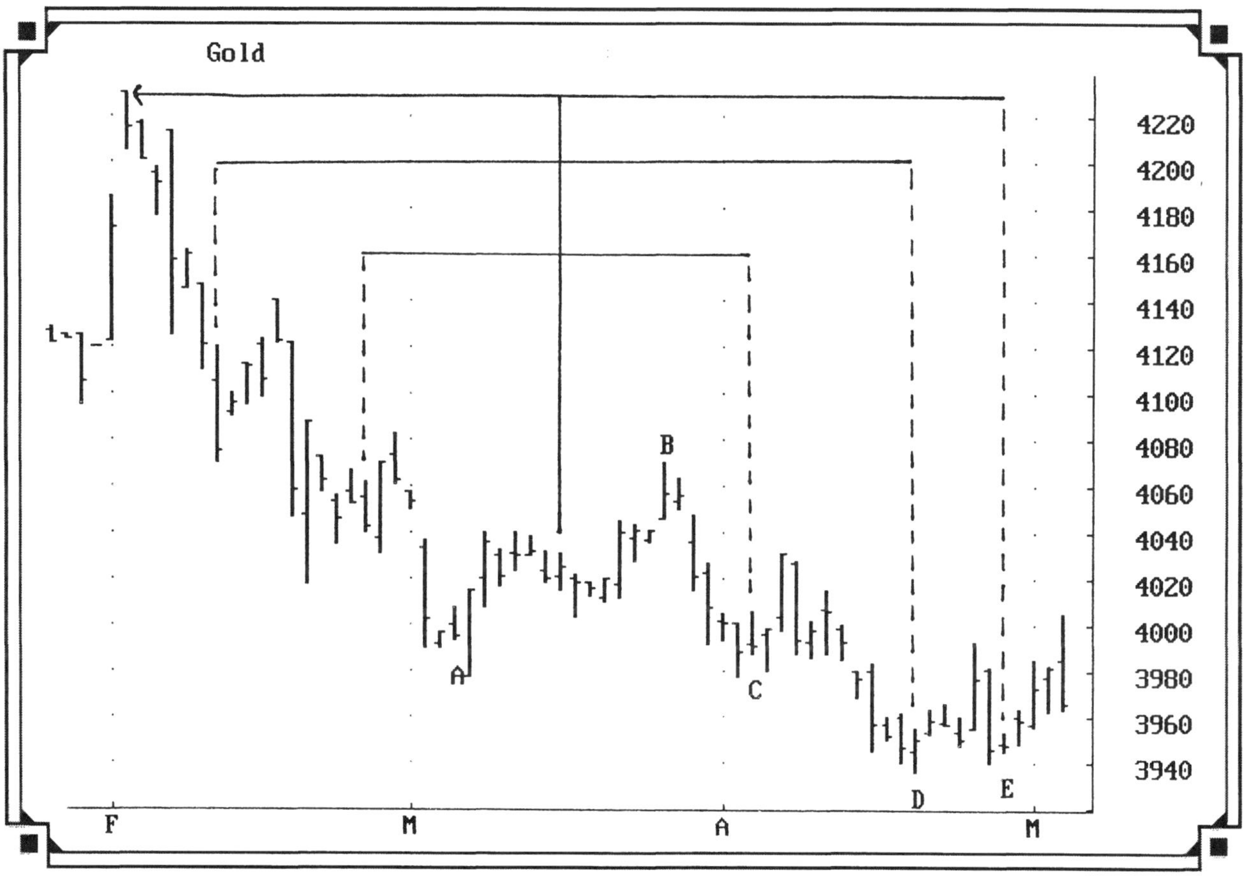

On this Gold chart, we identify the reaction swing as (A) and (B). We start with the low close of the reaction swing and apply the reverse count. We discover low closes on the 6th, 17th, and a high of the upward trend on the 23rd day. Therefore, with the reverse count, we can project Reversal Days on April 3, April 19 , and April 29, marked as (C), (D), (E) on the chart.

Reaction Cycle
Example 8

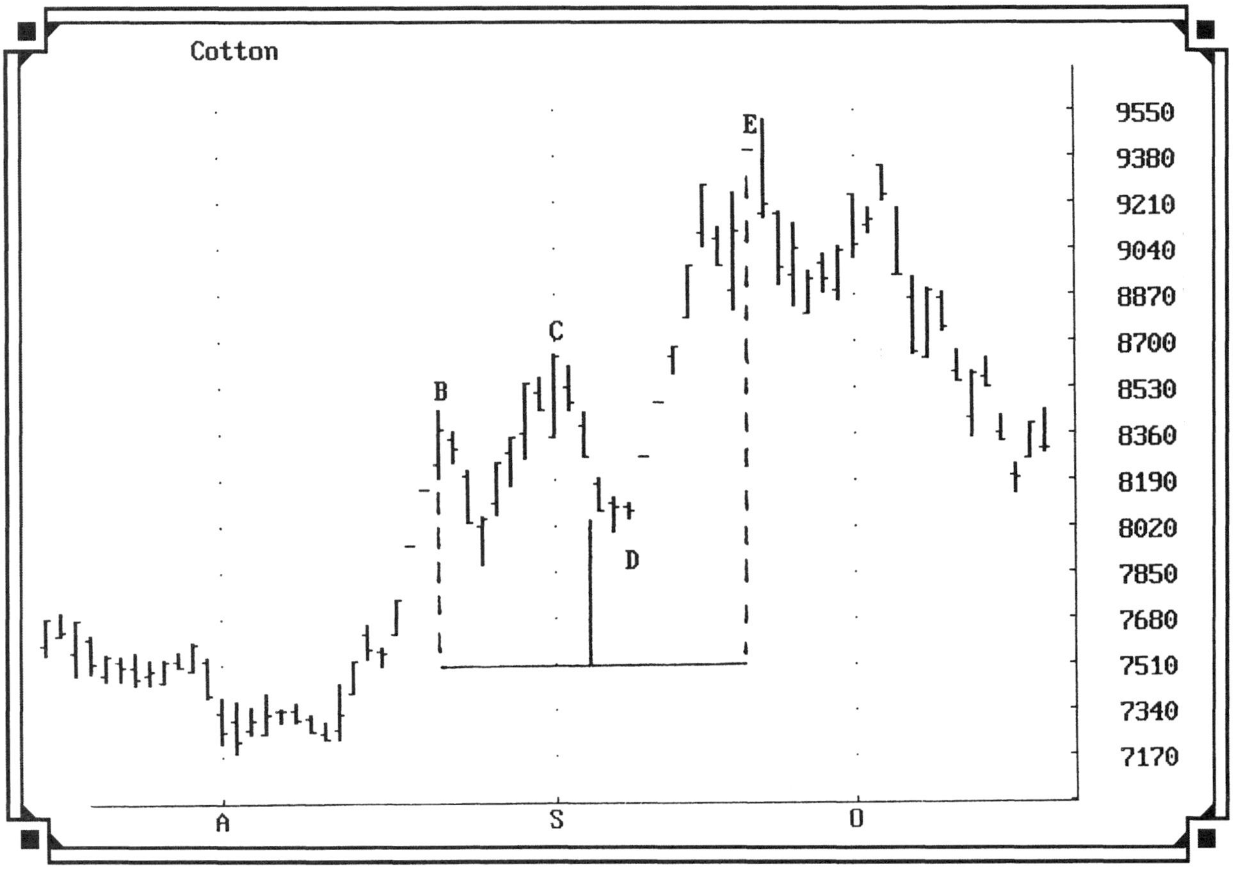

On this chart, (C) and (D) mark the reaction swing. Applying the reverse count, we find the high close on the 8th day. After counting forward an equal amount of days, we project a Reversal Day on September 21, marked as (E) on the chart. This projected Reversal Day proved to be a top in the Cotton.

Reaction Cycle
Example 9

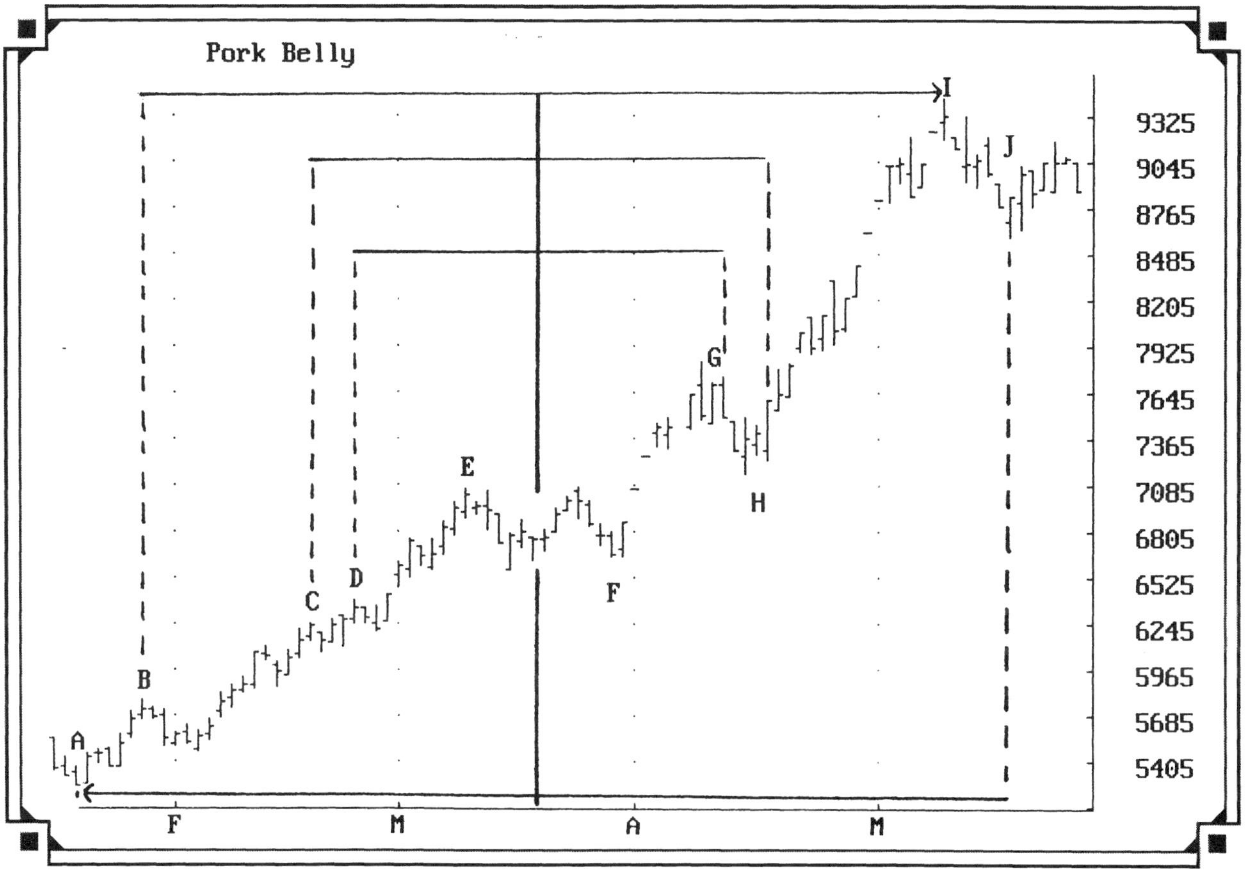

This Pork Bellies chart demonstrates how small reactions in the reverse count can identify small reactions in the forward count. Points (E) and (F) mark the reaction swing. From the low close of this reaction swing, the reverse count identifies high closes on the 10th, 19th, and 29th day. The low close on the previous downtrend is on the 36th day. Using the forward count, we project April 11, marked (G), and April 17, marked (H) as Reversal Day. May 9, (I) and May 17 (J) are also projected as Reversal Days.

Chapter 9

REVERSAL DAY SIGNALS

Now that we know how to spot a Reversal Day through the forward and reverse count, it is time to explore the theory and concept behind our Reversal Day confirmation patterns.

Reversal Signals

Reversal Patterns are simply counter-directional price moves. In other words, Reversal Patterns put us into the market at a point when the market price is expected to reverse into the opposite direction. When market prices *advance* into the Reversal Day, we expect the market to *reverse into a declining* market price action. Similarly, when market prices *decline* into a Reversal Day we look for the market to *increase* after it reverses.

To isolate and predict the Reversal Day, we need three essential and interdependent ingredients: reversal dates, price patterns, and support and resistance prices. Briefly, this is how they work together:

In order for us to determine the Reversal Day, we look for a three to four day *setup* of price actions based on the previous days' open and close. Once the setup occurs, we watch the *signal days* for a pattern to form. The first signal day, called *the Reversal Day,* we expect the market to reverse; the second day, *called the Trail Day,* indicates which direction the market will move.

What You Should Know About Reversal Signals

1. Reversal Patterns are characterized as a counter-directional price move.
   - If prices advance into the Reversal Day, the price action is expected to reverse and the market declines.
   - If the price declines into a Reversal Day, the price action is expected to reverse and the market increases.
2. All Reversal Day patterns involve three to four setup days.
   - The two days preceding the Reversal Day, called signal days, indicate which pattern is forming.
3. Confirmation for the Reversal Day will occur on one of two consecutive days.
   - Day One--Reversal Day; the day the market reverses
   - Day Two--Trail Day; indicates the future market direction
4. Before deciding upon a strategy, check the previous day's open and close prices.
   - A higher close means the market closed higher than the opening price.
   - A lower close means the market closed lower than the opening price.
5. Reversal Days are interdependent upon three factors...
   - Reversal dates
   - Price patterns
   - Support and resistance areas.

Reversal Day Terms

***Price Patterns**: based on how the market opens and closes compared to the previous day.*

***Higher Close**: the market closes higher than the opening price.*

***Lower Close**: the market closes lower than the opening price.*

***Reversal Day**: the day the market reverses direction.*

***Trail Day:** the day following the Reversal Day. The Trail Day often indicates the future market direction.*

***Price Advances into a Reversal Day:** the market price is going up into a projected Reversal Day. On Reversal Day the price reverses into the opposite direction so we expect a price decline.*

***Price Declines into a Reversal Day**: the market price is going down into a projected Reversal Day. On Reversal Day the price reverses into the opposite direction so we expect a price increase.*

***Reversal Day Techniques**: A system by which six different confirmation patterns are used in conjunction with reversal dates and support and resistance signals. This technique projects a market reversal and direction.*

***Reversal patterns**: Three confirmation patterns of the Reversal Day Technique used in elimination sequence to project a market reversal. Each pattern has its own criteria for entering or exiting the market.*

***Continuation patterns:** Three less common confirmation patterns of the Reversal Day Technique. All three patterns are used independently of each other to determine a price move that will follow the same direction as the current trend. Continuation patterns usually develop at support and resistance levels and have their own criteria for entering or exiting the market.*

***Confirming Signals**: Six price patterns used to confirm Reversal Day signals. These patterns will 'setup' three to four trading days before the Reversal Day. The two days leading up to the Reversal Day confirm which of the six patterns are forming. The confirmation of a signal occurs only on one of two consecutive days; the Reversal Day or the Trail Day.*

***Range**: Determined by subtracting the previous day's high from the previous day's low.*

***Setup days:** Two days prior to the Reversal Day when pattern conditions form to favor trading.*

Chapter 10

THREE TRADE SECRETS

In this chapter we review the specific rules for the three Reversal Patterns. Also included are some examples of each type of pattern. We recommend you go step-by-step with us through each example for they represent the key to confirming the Reversal signals.

The three Reversal Patterns we will discuss are:

- *Major Reversals* (Pattern One)
- *New High/New Low* (Pattern Two)
- *Trail Day* (Pattern Three)

Reversal Day Patterns

The three Reversal Day patterns seek and uncover signals that other patterns simply cannot find because each has its own talent to spot a Reversal Day and Trail Day. They work like a sort of safety net because they line up *consecutively*, waiting for a turn to spot a Reversal Day. If the first pattern does not 'catch' the signal, the second kicks in. If the second fails, the third pattern is available. *Therefore, we do not use these patterns <u>with</u> each other. Rather, these patterns help to '<u>eliminate</u>' each other as options.*

Always check the criteria for a *Major Reversal (Pattern One)* first. These four rules are listed on Page 86. If any of the conditions fail to develop, go on to *New High/New Low (Pattern Two).* If necessary, follow the same procedure for the *Trail Day (Pattern Three).* Finally, always put the 'stops' where suggested. This prevents you from becoming emotionally involved and protects against hasty decisions.

While exploring these patterns, regularly refer to each pattern's *What You Should Know* page. Learn all three patterns intimately. Notice the differences and the similarities of each. Eventually, the market's fluctuation will not fool you. Instead, you will be excited at the possibilities of applying one of these patterns.

REVERSAL DAY PATTERNS

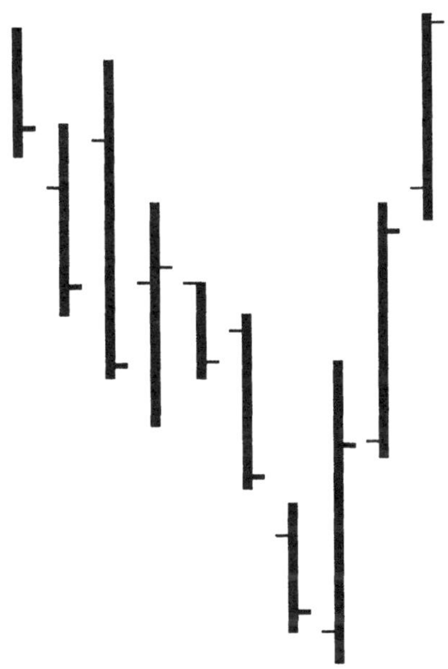

Pattern One: Major Reversals

What You Should Know About

Pattern One: Major Reversals

1. On the *setup* days, (two days prior to the Reversal Day), look for an advancing market with higher closes.

2. On the *Reversal Day*, look for the opening price to be equal to, or higher than, the closing price of the previous day.

3. A confirmed sell signal occurs when the market trades below 62% of the previous day's range.

4. Place protective stops above the high on sell signals, (or below the low on buy signals). These price levels should hold if it is a good signal.

(Reverse all rules to confirm buys in declining markets)

Pattern One: Major Reversals
Example 1

On the next example, Hogs traded lower because of a bearish report. Two days leading into the Reversal Day, (setup days), it fell sharply lower. Both days closed lower than the opening price for that day.

On the Reversal Day, the market opened lower. After hitting a new low, selling dried up and the market started to rally. At the end of the day, the market closed higher than the previous day's high. This confirmed a reversal in the market. (Remember, with this pattern, the market only has to rally more than 62% of the previous day's range).

This trade experienced an open profit at the end of the day. As you can see, the low of the Reversal Day held and the market continued to rally for the next two weeks.

Pattern One: Major Reversals

Example 1

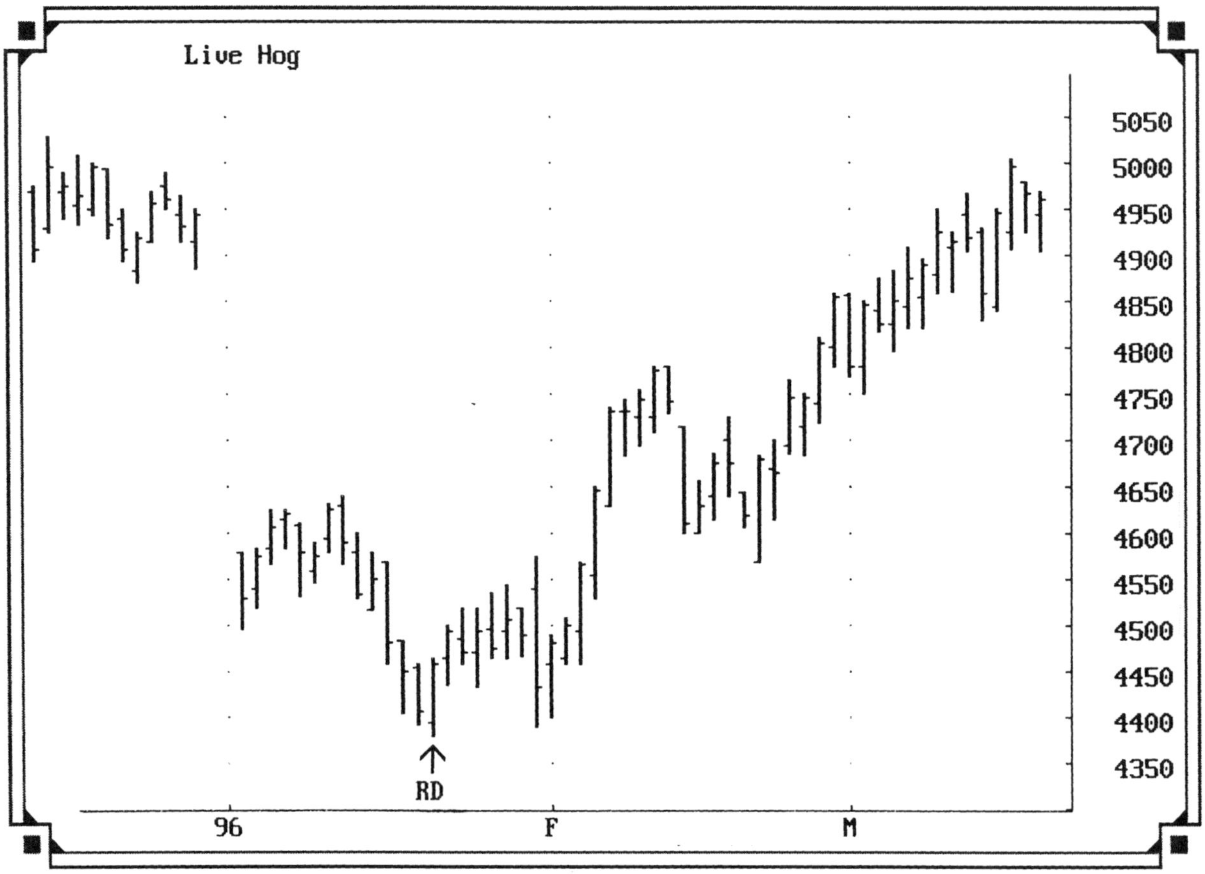

Pattern One: Major Reversals
Example 2

Note in this S&P 500 chart that the contract high set on December 14 was tested on January 3. The market closed higher than the opening prices of the days leading into the Reversal Day (scheduled for January 4th) on both of these days.

On the Reversal Day, the market opened higher and quickly made a new contract high of 635.40. This high took out the old high by 35 points. Afterward, it reversed its trend and started to trade lower. This confirmed the reversal.

Following the confirmation of this pattern, the market fell over 3,000 points in only five days. You should also notice the Reversal pattern on October 27. This was the beginning of a strong rally.

Pattern One: Major Reversals
Example 2

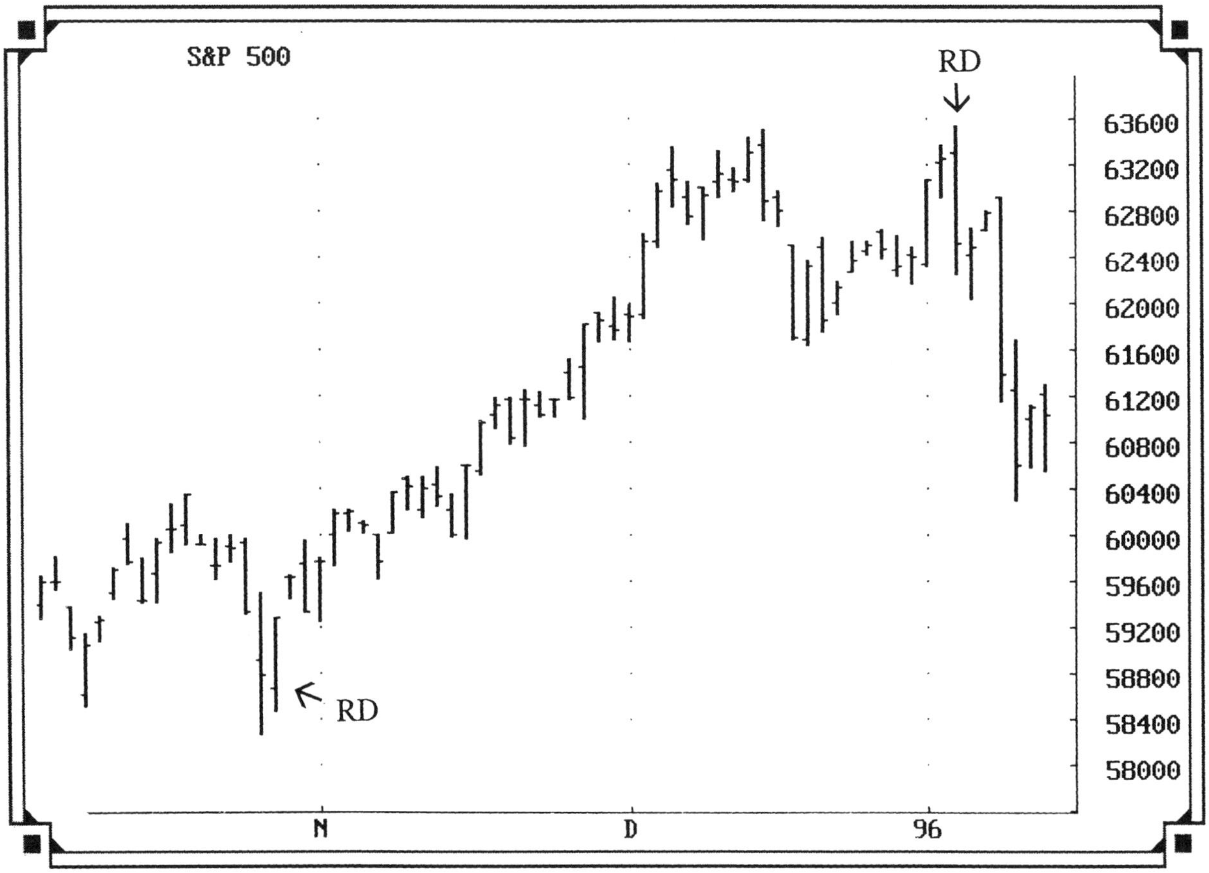

Pattern One: Major Reversals
Example 3

Notice on example 3 that Coffee experienced a strong downward trend for over a month. It appeared to hit a bottom. However, after a weak rally that lasted five days, the market made a sharp break and tested the previous low. Both of the days leading into the Reversal Day closed lower (the market closed lower than the opening price). On the Reversal Day, the market opened lower, making new contract lows. It looked like another down day, but the selling disappeared and the market rallied to finish the day sharply higher. The Major Reversal pattern formed on September 17 when the market then moved higher for four days. Once the Reversal pattern began, the market turned down for four consecutive days. Once again, another reversal pattern formed. This last turn sent Coffee into a nine day rally.

On each of the three Reversal patterns just shown, the lows on the buy patterns and the highs on the sell patterns all hold without penetration. Most of the time this will be true, though not every time.

Pattern One: Major Reversals
Example 3

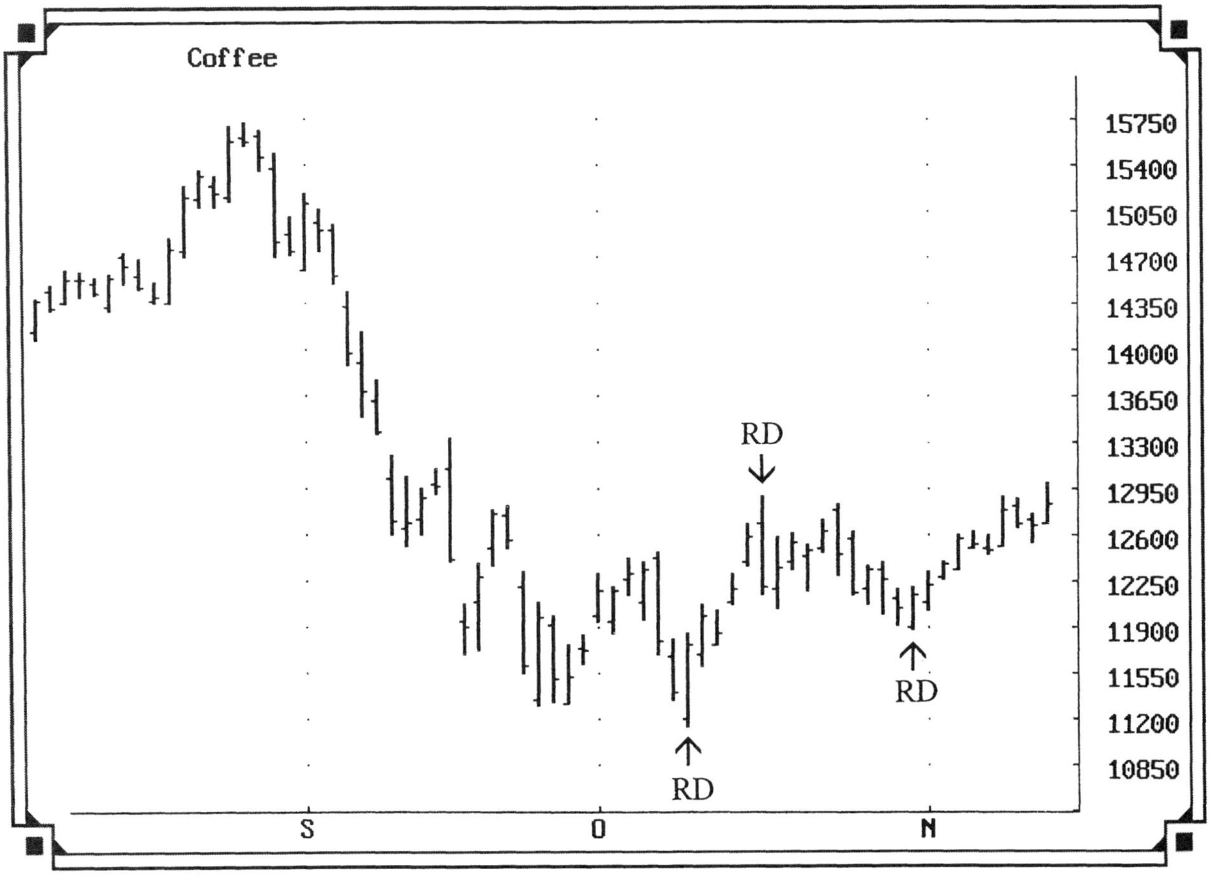

We recommend placing stops above the highs and below the lows. Give the market at least 5 ticks before placing stops.

REVERSAL DAY PATTERNS

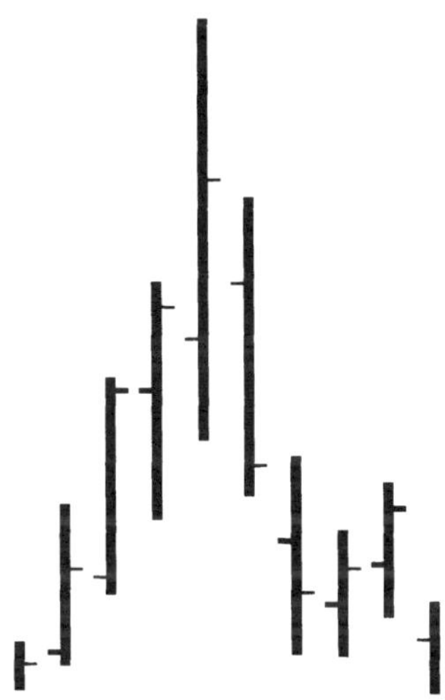

Pattern Two: New High/New Low

What You Should Know About

Pattern Two: New High/New Low

1. Look for an advancing market. Two days prior to the Reversal Day the market should close higher, i.e., the closing price is higher than the opening price.

2. On the Reversal Day, look for the market to also close higher than the opening price.

   - Always check that a Major Reversal (Pattern One) is not occurring before proceeding to step three.

3. On the Trail Day, the day after the Reversal Day, place a sell stop below the Reversal Day's low.

4. If the Reversal Day's low is not taken out on the Trail Day, determine the next move from the market closing:

   - If the market is going to close lower than the opening price, sell M.O.C. (market on close).

   - If the close is too proximate to determine, wait for the market to settle. The confirmation of a sell signal indicates the trader should sell the following morning.

(Reverse all rules to confirm buys in declining markets)

Pattern Two: New High/New Low
Example 1

In example 1, Pork Bellies traded lower for several days after a bearish report. Two days prior to the Reversal Day the market closed lower than the opening price. On the Reversal Day the market opened *higher* than the previous day's close, therefore a Major Reversal (Pattern One) was *not* forming.

We wait for the Trail Day (the next day) to see if a signal develops. On the Reversal Day, the market closed lower than the opening price. This indicated a possible signal on the Trail Day.

On January 22, the market traded higher than the Reversal Day high. New High/New Low buy signal was confirmed.

The market rallied for several weeks thereafter.

Pattern Two: New High/New Low
Example 1

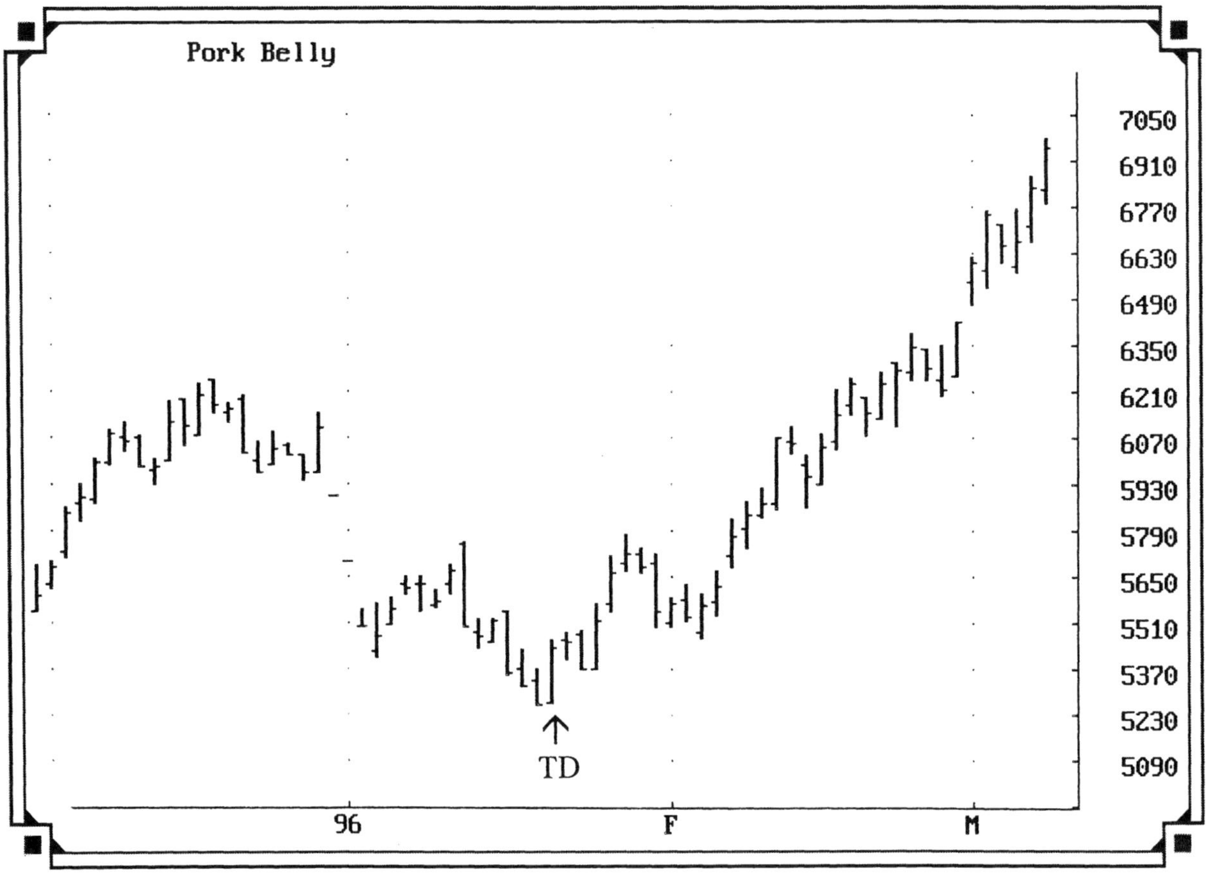

Pattern Two: New High/New Low Reversals
Example 2

In example 2, Coffee traded higher for five days against the main trend. Two days leading into the Reversal Day, the market closed higher than the opening price. On December 12, the Reversal Day, the market experienced a narrow range day and closed higher than the opening price.

On the Trail Day, the market opened lower and quickly traded below 104.90. This confirmed the sell signal because it traded below the low of the Reversal Day. The high of the Reversal Day held. The market continued a sharp downtrend for the next nine days.

Coffee fell over 1,400 points before traveling into the next Reversal Day.

Pattern Two: New High/New Low Reversals
Example 2

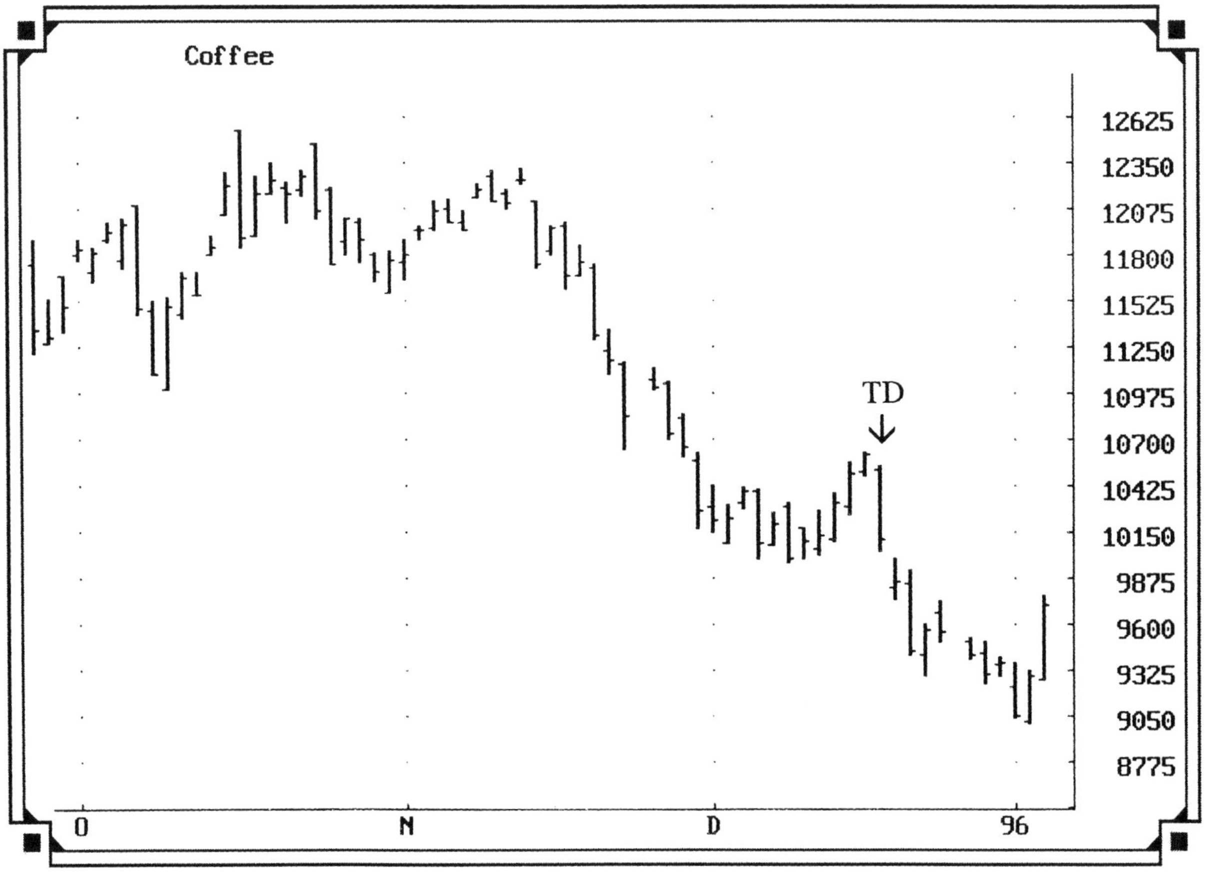

Pattern Two: New High/New Low Reversals
Example 3

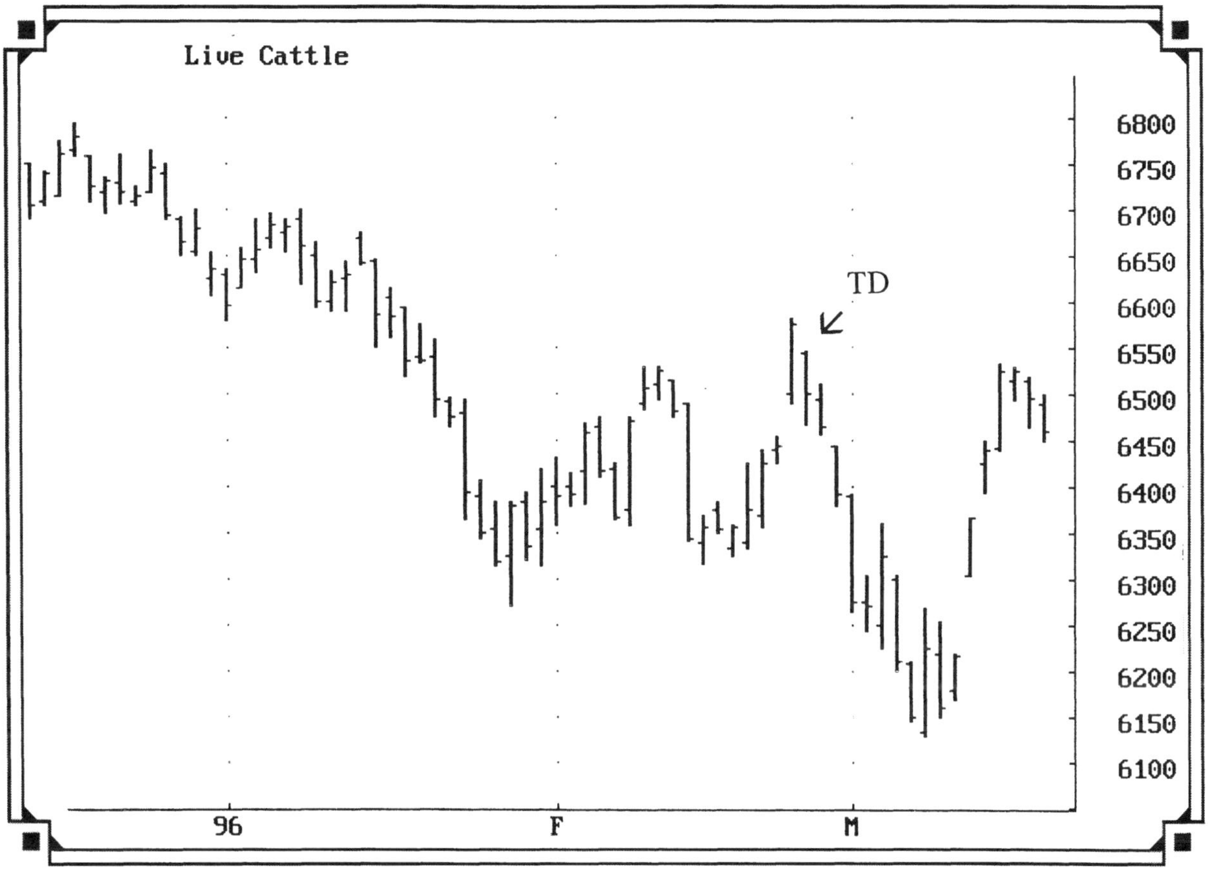

Cattle were in an overall downward trend when the market rallied against the trend and took out the previous high. Two days previous to the projected Reversal Day, the market closed higher than it opened. On the projected Reversal Day, the market also closed higher than it opened. A New High/New Low pattern may be forming. On the Trail Day, the market opened lower and continued lower. It took out the previous day's low which confirmed a sell signal. Cattle continued to drop for the next eight days resulting in a 350 point move down.

REVERSAL DAY PATTERNS

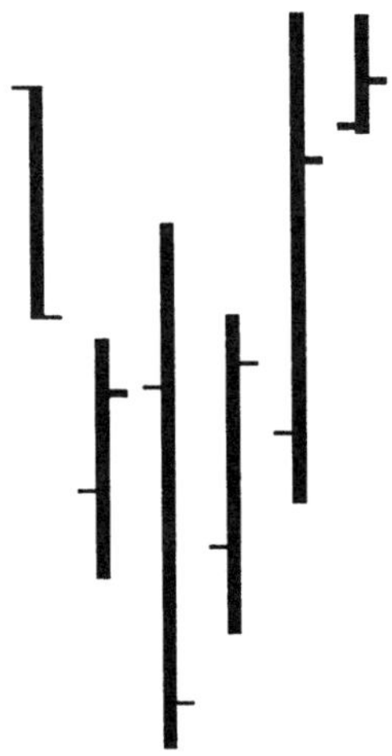

Pattern Three: Trail Day

What You Should Know About

Pattern Three
Trail Day

1. If *Pattern One* or *Pattern Two* fails to develop, look for a *Trail Day* (*Pattern Three*) price signal.
   - The market trades *higher* on *either* the Reversal Day or the Trail Day than it did the day *before* the Reversal Day.

2. Sell M.O.C. (market on close) if you know the market will close lower than the opening price of the Trail day.
   - If the signal is not confirmed at the market close, wait for the market to settle.
   - If you receive a confirmed signal, sell at the market the next morning.

(Reverse all rules to confirm buys in declining markets)

Pattern Three: Trail Day

Example 1

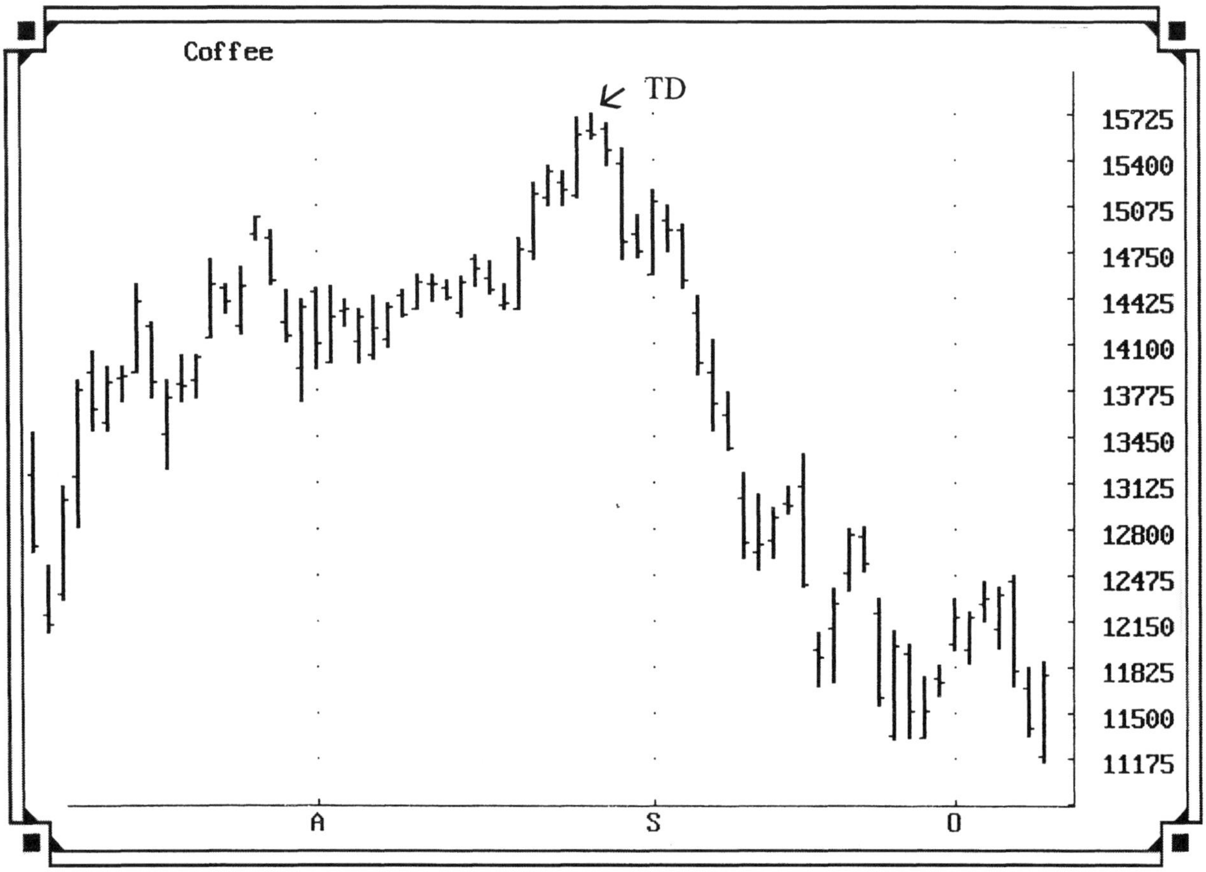

In this first example, Coffee traded higher into the Reversal Day. However, the markets closed opposite each other on the two days before the Reversal Day so a setup pattern was not confirmed. The Trail Day opened higher before pushing lower to close lower than the opening price. This confirmed a sell signal. The closing price of the Trail Day showed the beginning of a long downward move in the coffee market. The Reversal Day marked the beginning of a move which lasted several weeks.

Pattern Three: Trail Day
Example 2

In this second example, Wheat traded lower into the predetermined date with no signal. Two days prior to the Reversal Day, *Pattern One* or *Pattern Two* criteria were not developing.

We waited for the Trail Day to indicate the next market direction. On the Trail Day the market opened steady. It quickly made a new low before it turned.

A strong rally followed which confirmed the *Trail Day* signal and indicated Wheat should be bought at the close. Wheat finished higher than the opening price and continued a strong rally.

Eventually it made new contract highs.

Pattern Three: Trail Day
Example 2

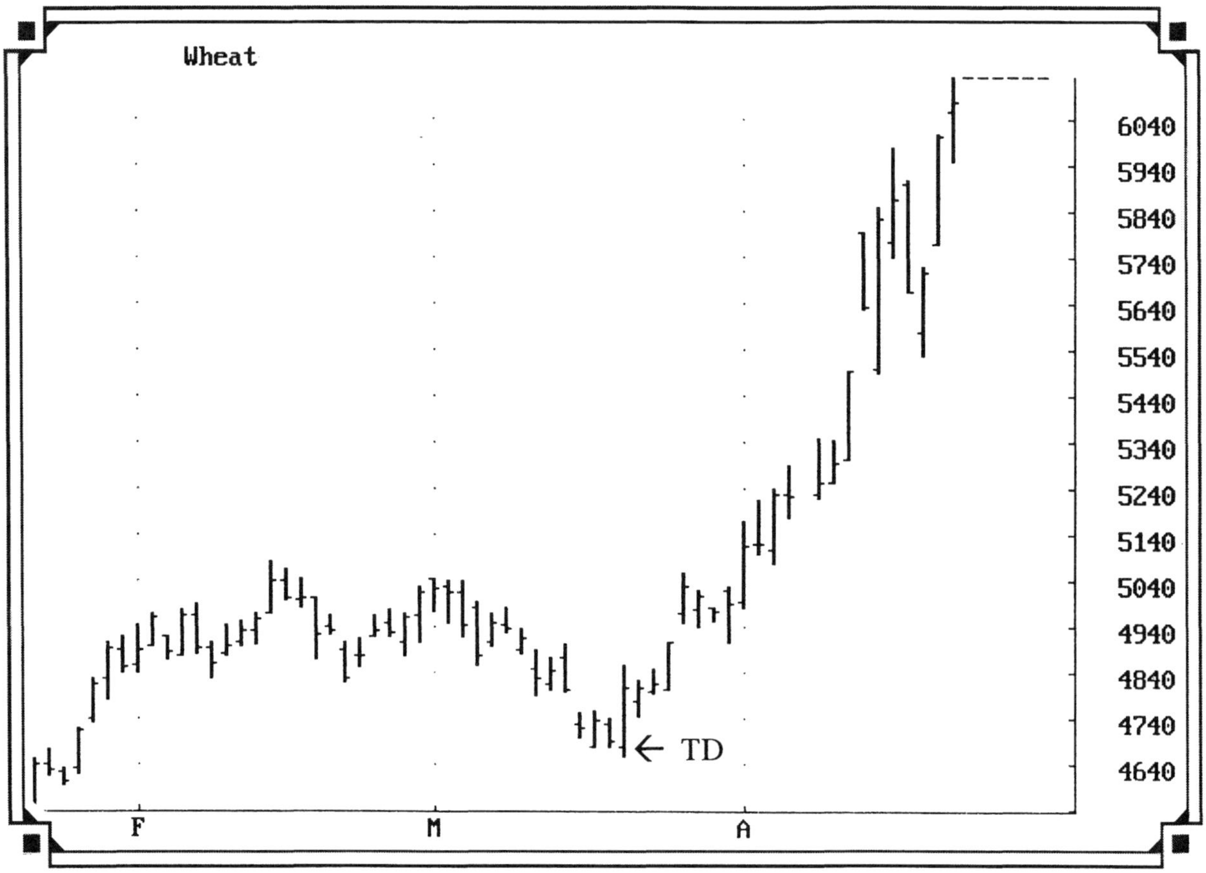

Chapter 11

CONTINUATION PATTERNS

In this chapter we feature the three *Continuation Patterns*. Although these patterns are not as common as Reversal Day patterns, their market potential is just as effective.

We again recommend you thoroughly examine the examples, the specific rules, investment signals and guidelines for protective stops.

The three Continuation Patterns are:

- *Gapping (*Pattern Four)
- *Strong Advance* (Pattern Five)
- *Trending (*Pattern Six)

Continuation Patterns

The market will not reverse every time there is a projected Reversal Day. Sometimes the market *continues with the trend.* Knowing when this will happen is just as important as knowing when to expect a market reversal. The patterns used to identify these trends are called *Continuation Patterns*

The Continuation Patterns tend to occur near support and resistance or consolidation areas. However, in order to isolate and predict a continuation pattern, we also need to know a Reversal Day and a confirming price pattern. These three patterns are designed to give you that confirming price pattern. Once the market price advances into a projected Reversal Day and a Continuation Pattern forms, we expect the market to continue in the same direction as the current trend.

While exploring these patterns, keep referring to the "What You Should Know" page. Knowing the setup for each pattern is very important because, unlike Reversal Day Patterns, the three Continuation Patterns work *independently* of each other and have their own kind of specific market environment. Once you learn all three patterns intimately, you will be excited at the possibilities presented by these patterns.

CONTINUATION PATTERNS

Pattern Four: Gapping

What You Should Know About

Pattern Four Gapping

1. The *Gapping Pattern*, (Pattern Four), occurs when the *market gaps* in the same direction as the current trend.

2. When this pattern occurs the market will usually continue in that direction for a minimum of two to three days.

3. On the Reversal Day, in an advancing market, the opening price is higher than the previous day's high. This leaves a price gap and the Gapping Pattern may be setting up.

4. If, by the end of the trading day, the gap does not fill then the continuation signal is confirmed. This usually indicates the current trend will continue for at least the next two or three days.

Reverse all rules to confirm sells in declining markets)

Pattern Four: Gapping
Example 1

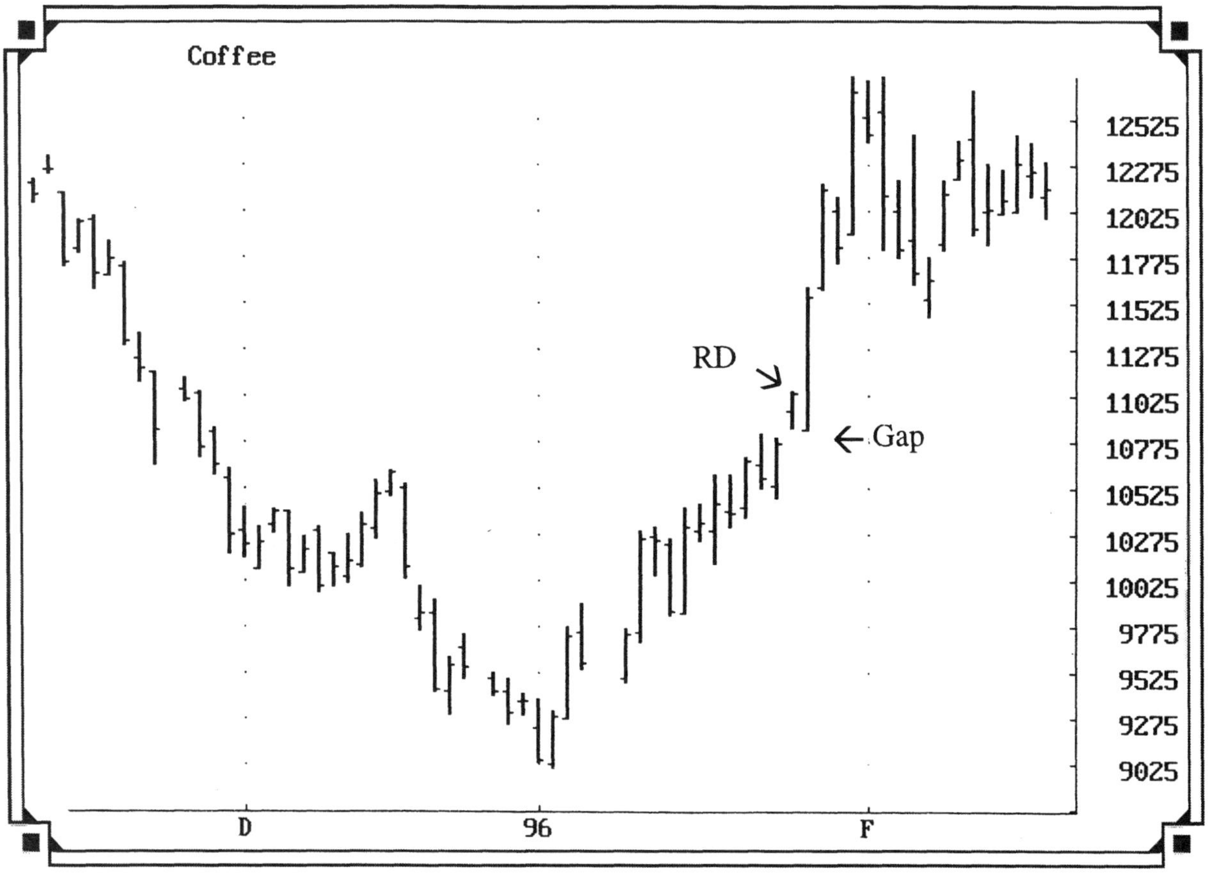

Coffee traded higher for several weeks. It then paused near a previous resistance area. The next day, the market gapped higher. It stayed higher the rest of that day, leaving a gap. The result was a market that moved sharply higher over the next four days.

Pattern Four: Gapping
Example 2

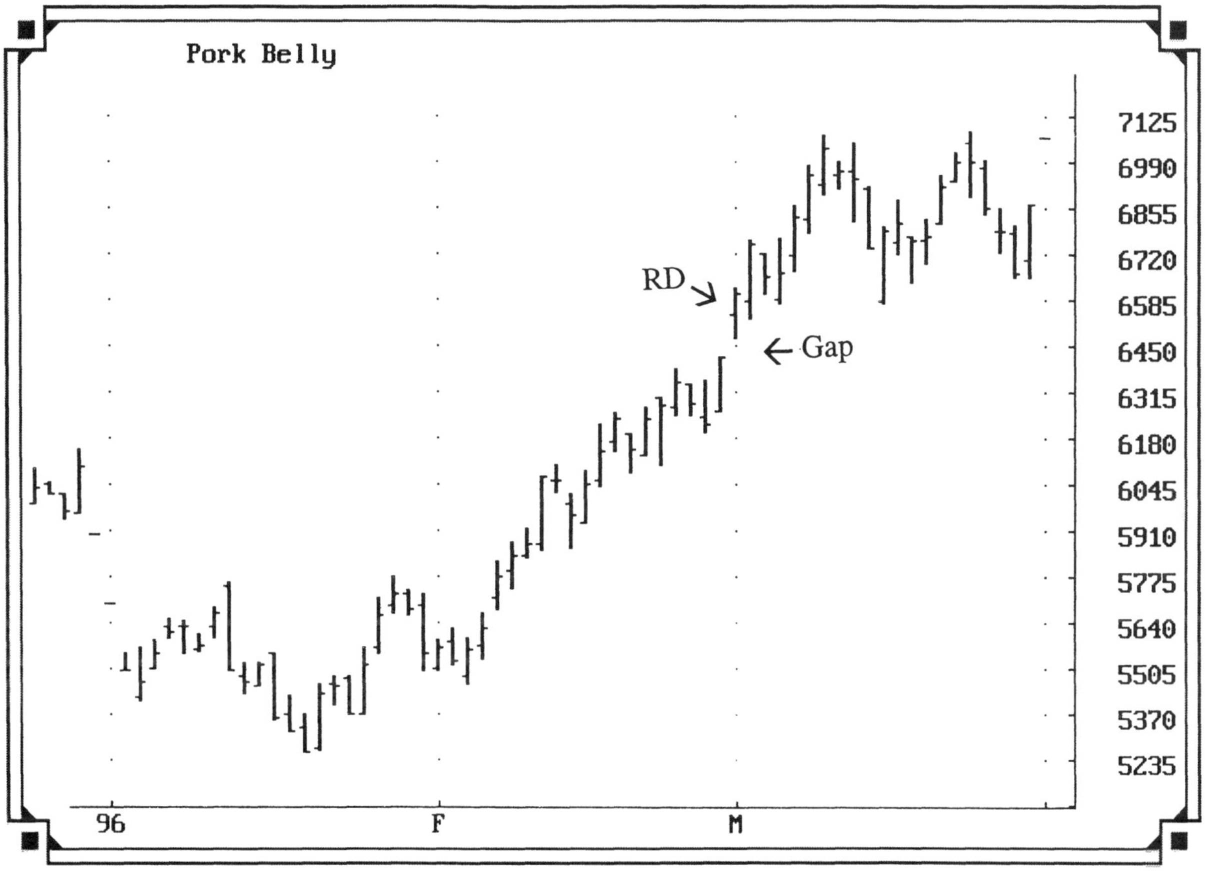

Example 2 shows that Pork bellies moved higher for several days. Just before the scheduled Reversal Day, the market pulled back for two days. On the day before the Reversal Day, the market moved higher and made a new high. Reversal Day, the market gapped higher on the opening and continued higher all day. This market never pulled back to fill the gap left from the opening. Instead, it continued higher for the next six days.

CONTINUATION PATTERNS

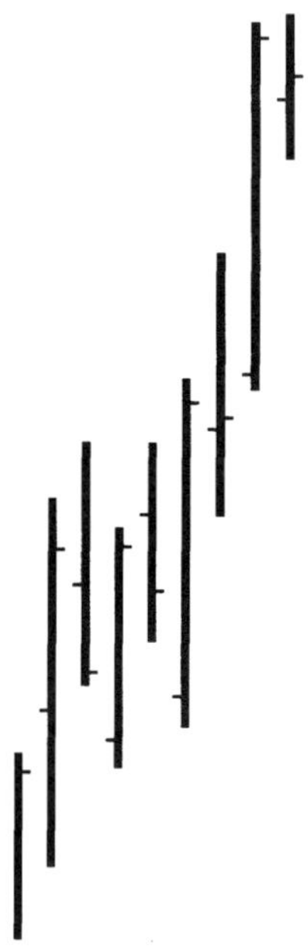

Pattern Five: Strong Advance

What You Should Know About

Pattern Five
Strong Advance

1. *Two days before the Reversal day* (setup days) the market *closes opposite*. In other words, in an advancing market, the market will close lower than the opening price on the setup days. This will be against the trend.

2. On the *day before the Reversal Day,* the market closes opposite. Opposite means that the closing price will be higher than the opening price and in the same direction as the trend.

3. On *Reversal Day* the market should *close in the same direction* as the first setup day. This indicates a lower closing price than the opening price which is against the trend.

4. *On the Trail day* place a buy stop above the high of the Reversal Day.

5. In this pattern, the first setup day and the Reversal day will always close against the current trend.

6. This pattern usually occurs after the market makes a strong advance and then consolidates. Often, a fast strong move follows this particular pattern.

Reverse all rules to confirm sells in declining markets)

Pattern Five: Strong Advance

Example 1

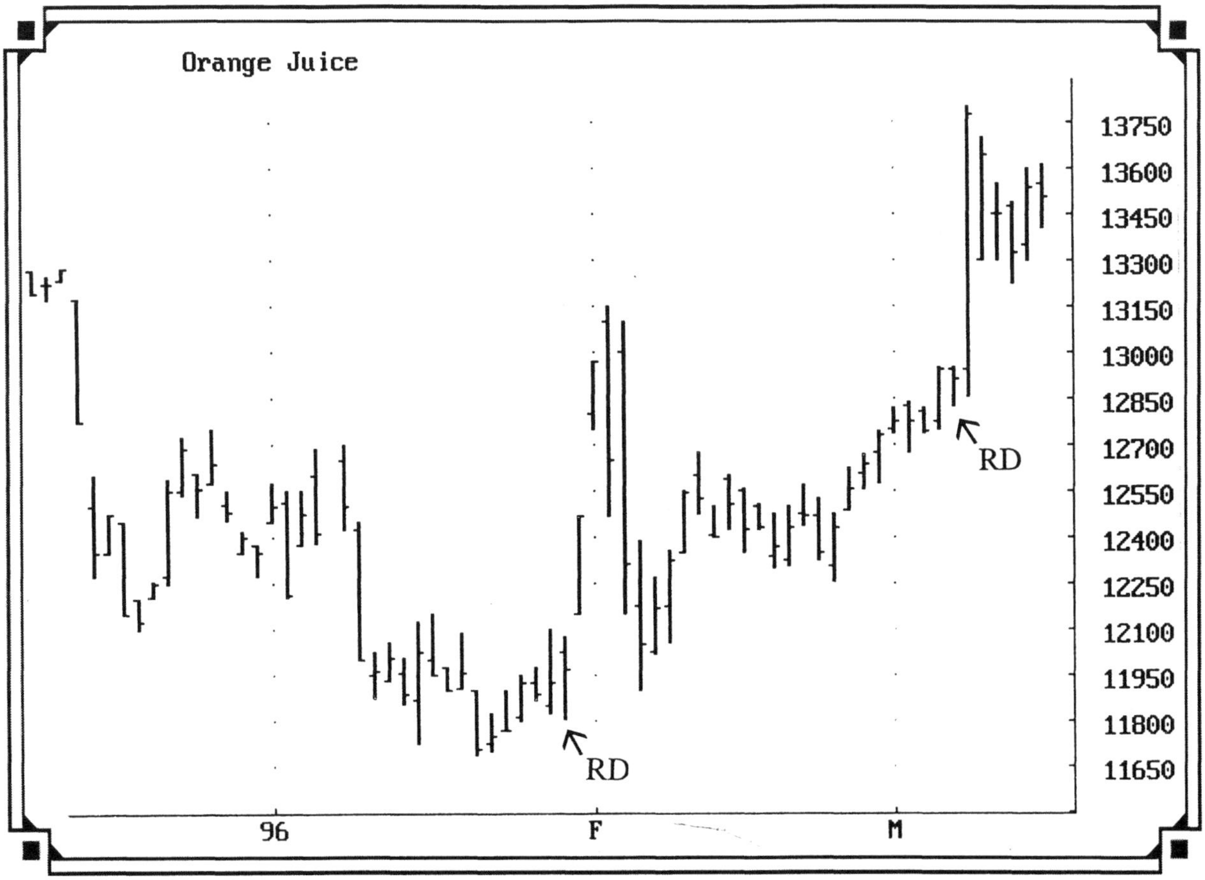

Orange Juice slowly traded higher when a Strong Advance Pattern (Five) formed. The first day closed lower than the opening price, meaning it was trending opposite. The second day closed higher than the opening price (same direction as the trend). The third day closed lower than the opening price (trending opposite). With this type of formation, a buy stop would be placed above the high of the third day. As you can see, the market opened higher and began a quick eight hundred point rally. This occurred again in Orange Juice about one month later. Another sharp rally resulted.

Pattern Five: Strong Advance
Example 2

In Example 2, the trend in Cotton was up and the market was in a correction. This Strong Advance pattern consisted of a day with a lower close, followed by a day with a higher close. On the third day the close was lower than the open. The market opened in the opposite direction of the overall trend.

A buy stop should be placed above the high of the third day, assuming this is the Reversal Day.

In this example, the market opened sharply higher and began a rally of over five hundred points.

Pattern Five: Strong Advance
Example 2

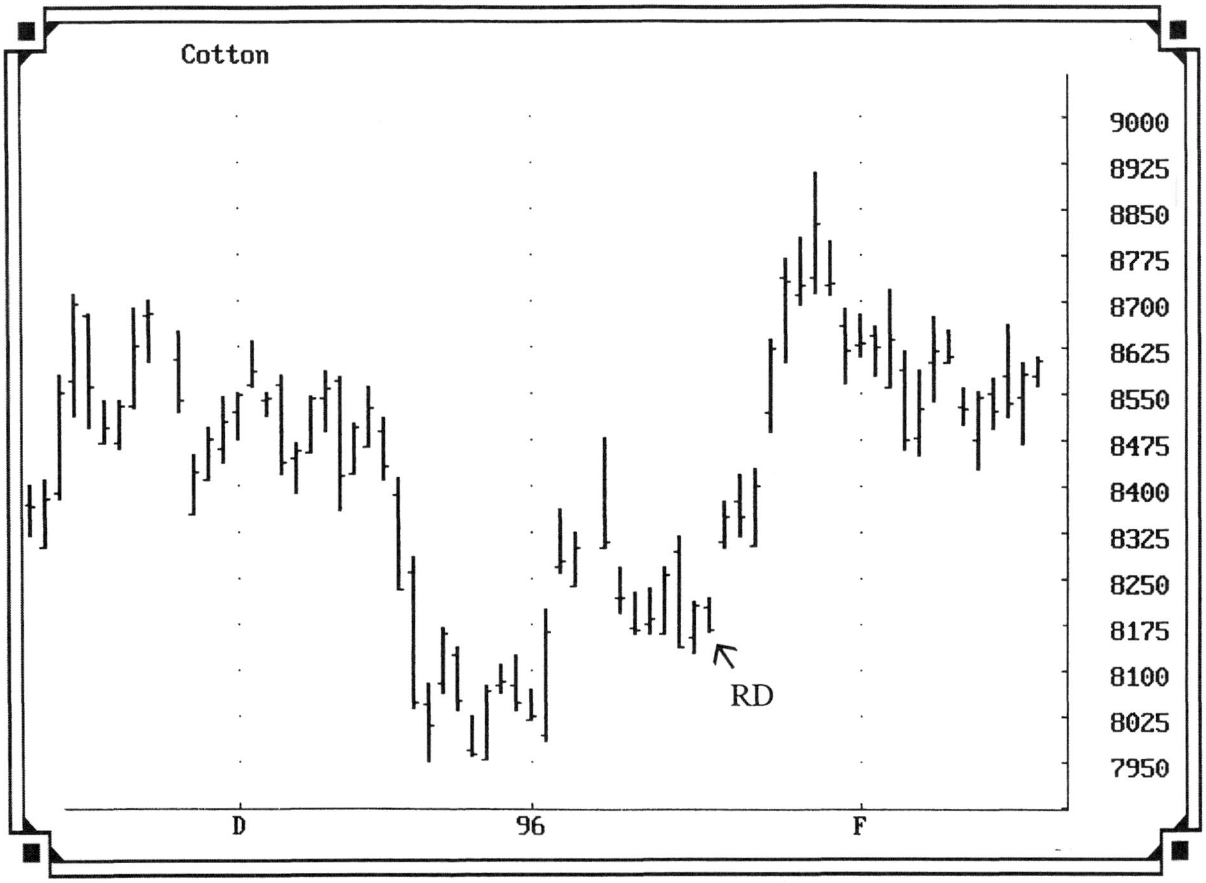

**Note:* *Reversal Days frequently mark the end of market corrections.*

CONTINUATION PATTERNS

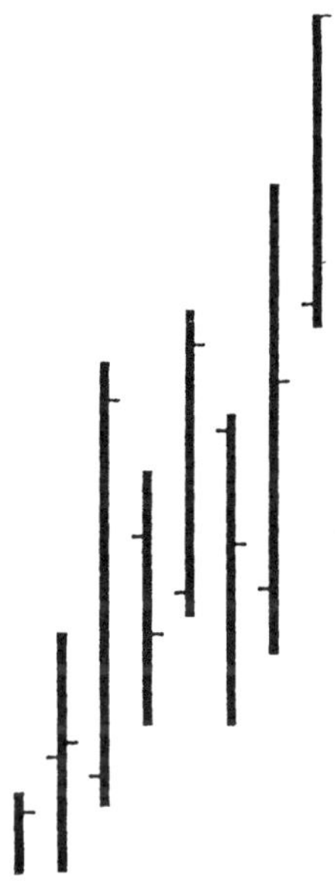

Pattern Six: Trending

What You Should Know About

Pattern Six Trending

1. This pattern is similar to the Strong Advance (Pattern Five) except the trend usually continues in a much more orderly fashion.

2. In an advancing market, look for a higher close than the opening price on the first setup day (two days prior to the Reversal Day). This should be in the same direction as the current trend.

3. One day before the Reversal Day, look for the market to close lower (closing price lower than opening price). This will be against the current trend.

4. On the Reversal Day, look for the market to close in the same direction as the first setup day (i.e., closing price higher than opening price). The trend also repeats itself (i.e., in the same direction as the current trend).

5. The market must close higher than the opening price to confirm a signal.

6. On the Trail Day, place a buy stop above the high of the Reversal Day.

(Reverse all to confirm sells in declining markets)

Pattern Six: Trending
Example 1

This first example of the Trending Pattern shows how the S&P 500 moved higher in a strong trend. As the market approached a resistance area, the Trending Pattern began to form.

The first day closed higher than the opening price and the trend was in the same direction. The next day, the market closed lower than the opening price and was trending opposite. On the third day, a projected Reversal Day, the market closed higher than the opening price. It was trending in the same direction.

The confirmation of the Trending Pattern came when the market traded higher than the high of the Reversal Day. Notice this same pattern occurred six days later, suggesting once again that the trend should continue higher.

Pattern Six: Trending
Example 1

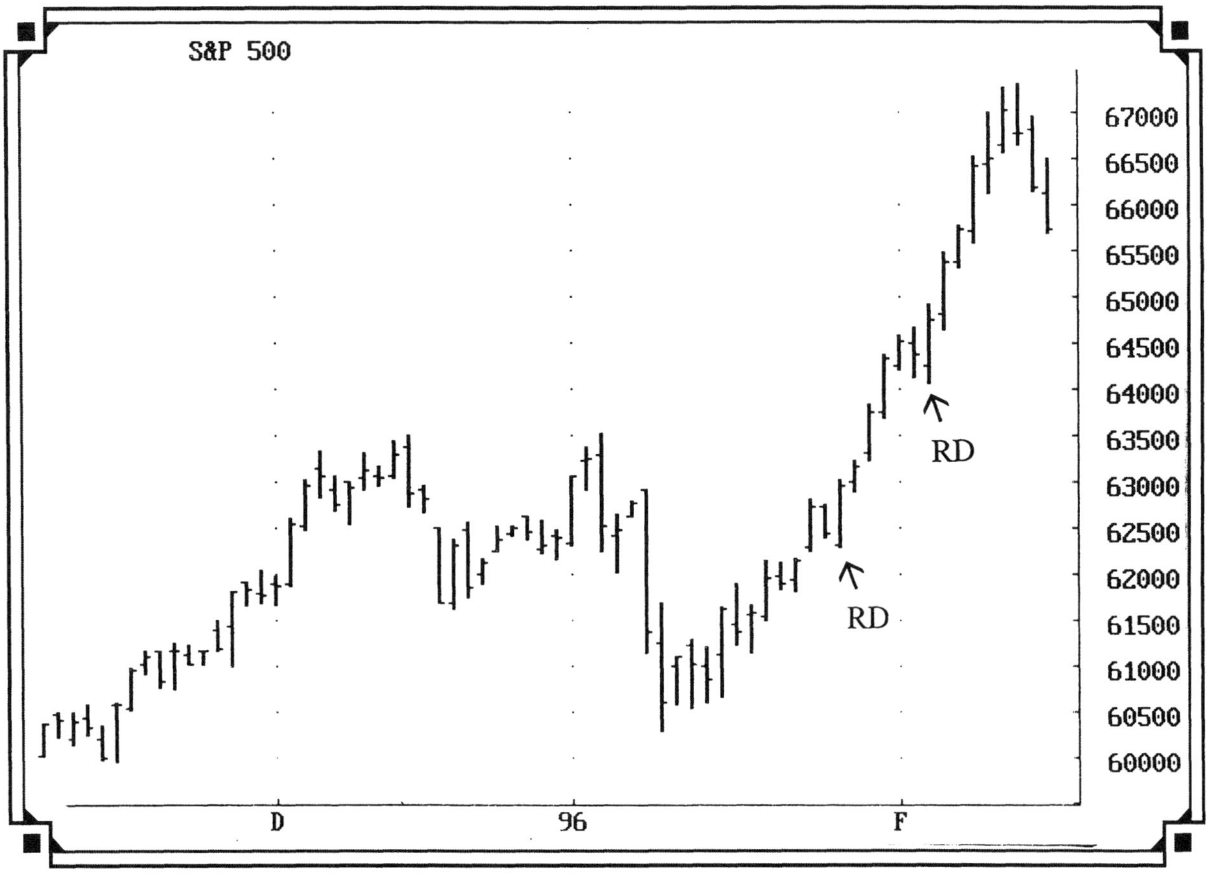

Pattern Six: Trending
Example 2

In this second Trending Pattern example we see how, after coming out of a week-long price retracement, the Crude Oil started to move higher. As it approached the previous high (resistance) the market formed a Trending Pattern.

With this type of formation, we will watch for the market to either move higher or reverse the trend and move lower. The market closed higher than the opening price on the first day. The following day, the market closed lower than the opening price. This indicated a need to watch for the Trending Pattern. The third day, the projected Reversal Day, the market closed higher than the opening price and in the same direction as the trend. This completed the pattern.

With this type of formation, a buy stop would be placed above the high of the third day.

Pattern Six: Trending
Example 2

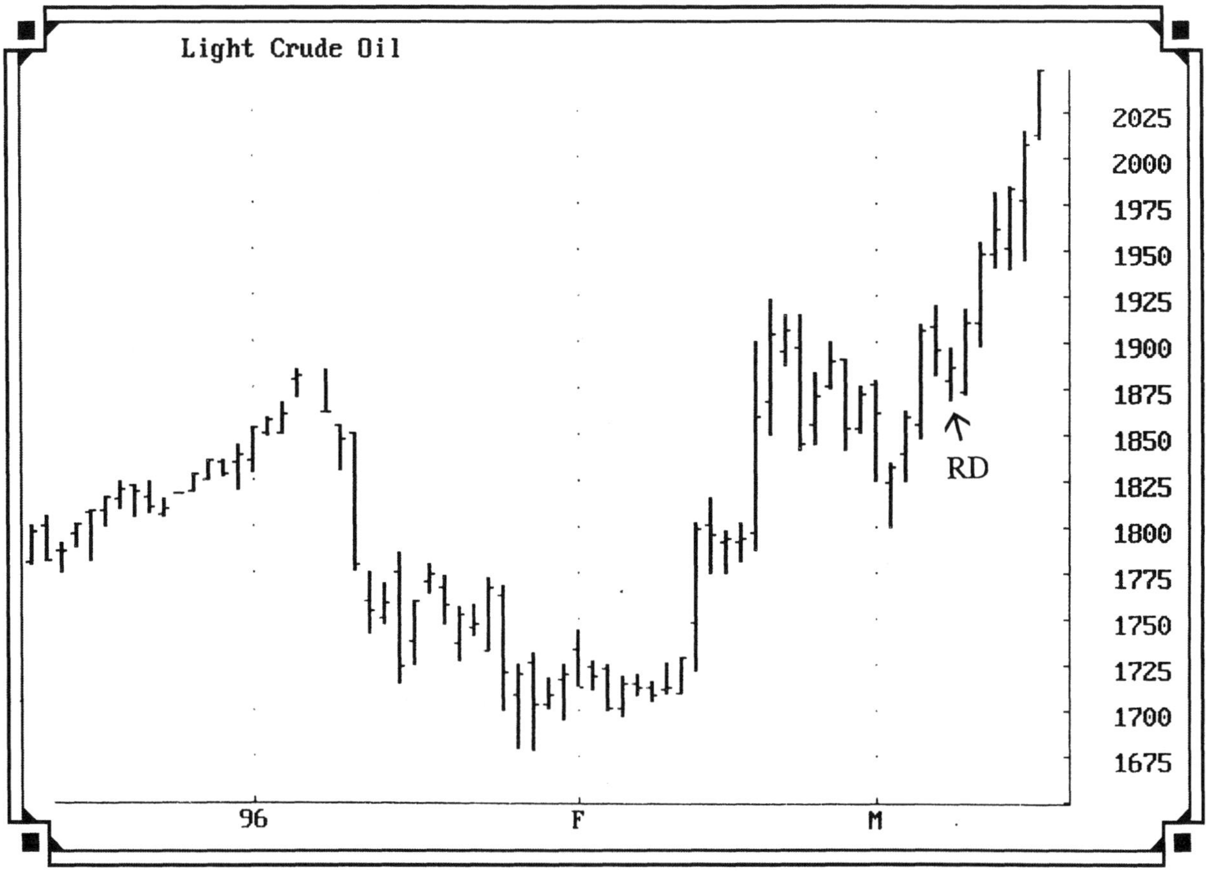

Chapter 12

TIME, PRICE AND PATTERNS COME TOGETHER

A lot has been written about the natural order of time and price in the markets and how they seem to work together in a natural cycle. Reversal dates and patterns also occur at natural support and resistance price levels. Once you witness how this is accomplished, the whole Reversal Day Technique is complete. In the next few chapters you will learn how the Reversal Day Technique uses patterns to blend with time and price signals. These signals, identified as Buy and Sell Windows, New Highs or New Lows, and the 20 Day Moving Average, are amazing when combined with our Reversal patterns.

Major Buy/Sell Window Signal

Using Major Buy and Sell Windows with our Reversal Day Technique is one of our favorite trading confirmation signals. Buy and Sell Windows occur when very specific retracements from an intermittent high/low lead to *very strong* moves in the market.

To take advantage of these market swings we must meet certain criteria. First, the retracement must be 60% of the original move (from the last high to low). Second, we must link it with the expected Reversal Day. Once these two factors setup, expect a Sell or Buy Window.

In the case of a Sell Window, the signal can occur anywhere between the retracement level and the high. When it is a Buy Window, the signal can occur anywhere between the retracement level and the low in conjunction with a Reversal Day. As an example, let's say the market establishes an intermediate high and is now retracing (trading lower) from that high. *Once the market retraces to 60% of the original move, it enters into a Buy Window.* If this corresponds to a predicted Reversal Day, we look for a pattern confirmation signal to enter long.

What You Should Know About

Spotting a Buy Window

1. Look for a *very specific* retracement from intermittent high/low. The retracement has to work in conjunction with the expected Reversal Day.

2. Once the market has retraced the 60%, it has entered into what we call a *Buy Window*.

3. If the market has retraced the 60% in conjunction with a scheduled Reversal Day, we will look for a signal to enter long.

(All Rules reversed for a Sell Window)

How to calculate a Buy Window

1. Once a market establishes an intermediate high and starts to move lower from this high, subtract the low (beginning of the upward trend) from the high. This equals the total range of the original move.

2. Now multiply the range by 60%.

3. Subtract that total from the high.

4. This equals the price level at which the *Buy Window* begins.

How to calculate a Sell Window

1. Once the market establishes an intermediate low and starts to move higher from this low, subtract the high from the low.

2. Multiply the range by 60%.

3. Add that number to the low.

4. This equals the price level at which the *Sell Window* begins.

Major Buy Window
Example 1

In the example on the next page, Copper hit a low of 109.30 on January 22 (A). The market went up to a high of 116.00 (B) on the rally that followed. Afterward, the market went into a correction and traded lower for the next seven days. On February 16 (C) the market hit a low of 110.60.

Now, let's calculate the Buy Window:

1. Subtract 109.30 (A) from 116.00 (B) to determine the range.
2. Multiply the range by 60%.
3. Subtract that total from 116.00 (B).
4. Your calculations should equal 111.98 (the beginning of the Buy Window).
5. Since Copper traded in 5 tick increments, round it off to 111.95.

Copper made a low of 110.60 during the correction which coincided with a projected Reversal Day. From this signal the markets moved higher over the next two weeks and never tested the low again.

Major Buy Window
Example 1

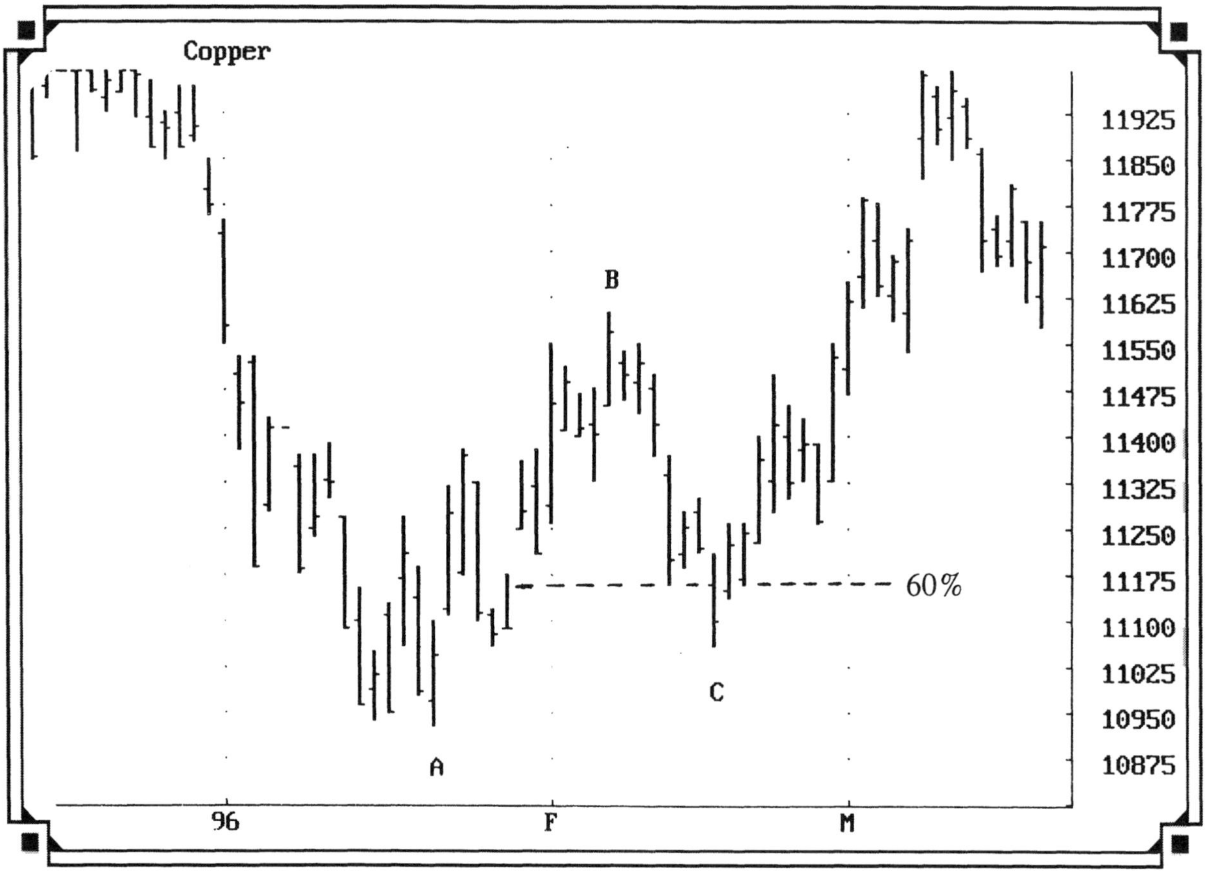

Major Sell Window
Example 1

Look at the example on the next page. Notice that Pork Bellies made a high of 64.80 (A) before the market traded lower then hit a low at 54.20 (B). Pork Bellies ended up trading as high as 62.50 before reversing and falling sharply lower (C).

Now let's calculate the Sell Window:

1. Subtract 64.80 (A) from 54.20 (B) to determine the range.
2. Multiply the range by 60%.
3. Add that number to the low of 54.20 (B).
4. The beginning of the Sell Window is 60.56

* *Note*: *The calculations for a Sell Window Pattern are the same as a Buy Window Pattern except they are based off of the low.*

Major Sell Window
Example 1

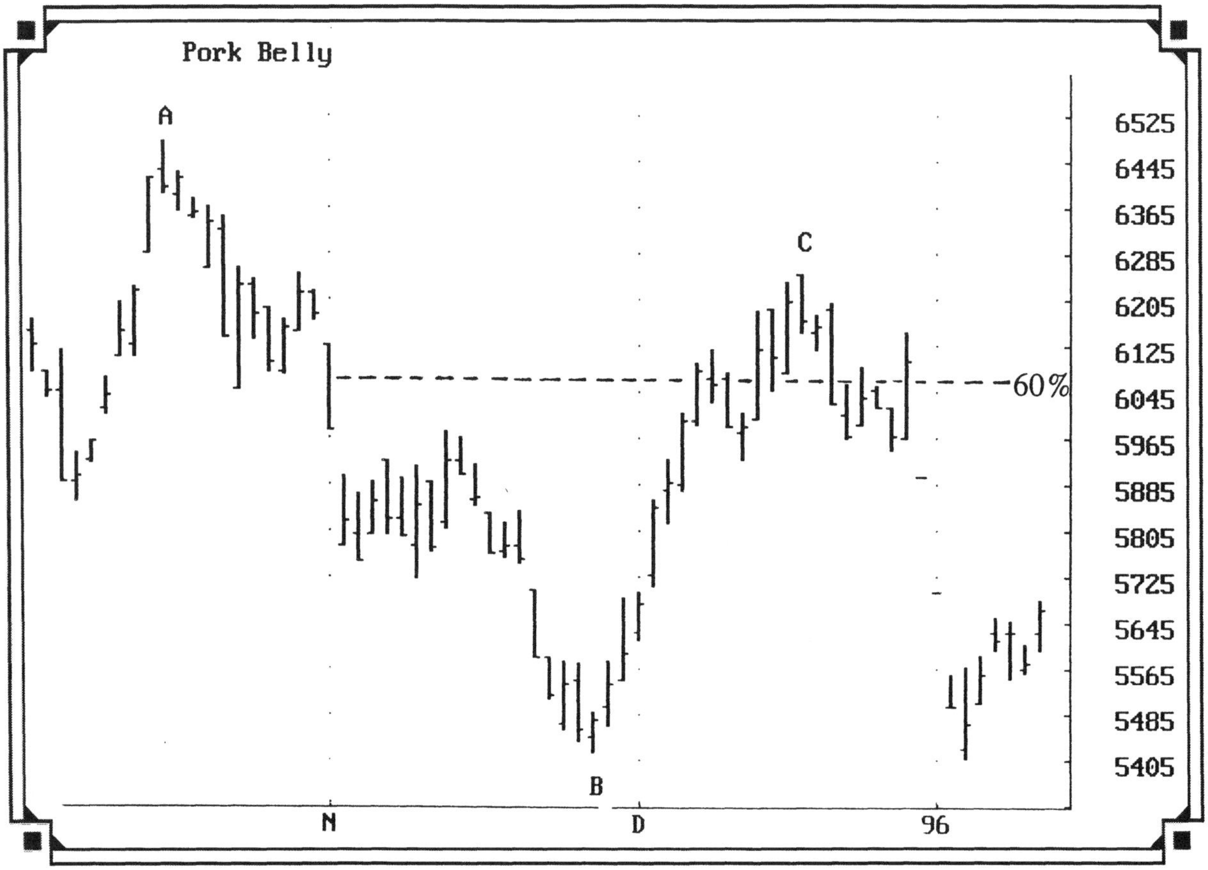

Minor Sell Leads To Major Buy Window
Example 1

In this example, the Minor Sell Window began the retracement down into a Major Buy Window.

Wheat made a low of 4.49 before reversing and trading higher (A). Wheat then made a high at 5.04 1/2 (B) before trading lower for five days (C). From this low the market traded higher than 60% of the recent downward move. This retracement put the market inside the Sell Window (D).

From this Sell Window, the market traded lower until it established a low inside the Major Buy Window on a projected Reversal Day (E).

Minor Sell Leads To Major Buy Window
Example 1

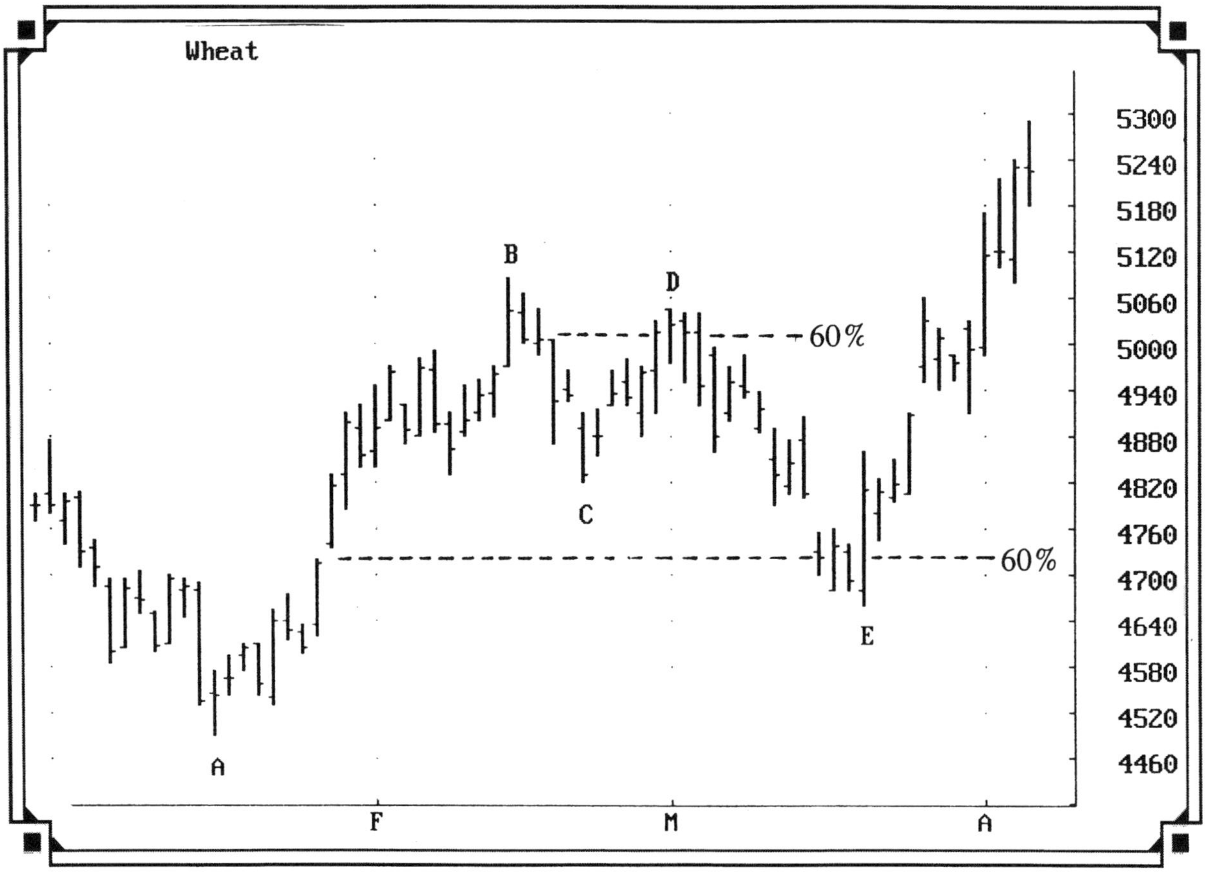

Major Buy Window
From Short Term Retracement
Example 1

Not all signals generated in a Buy or Sell Window occur after a long-term trend. This chart shows a Major Buy signal generated after a short-term retracement. Silver made a major low of 5.15 (A). After this low, the market traded higher for the next eight days. At (B), the market made a high at 5.27. The Buy Window started at 5.20. The market ended up making a low of 5.18 in conjunction with a projected Reversal Day (C). After this signal, a sharp rally of over 50 cents followed.

Chapter 13

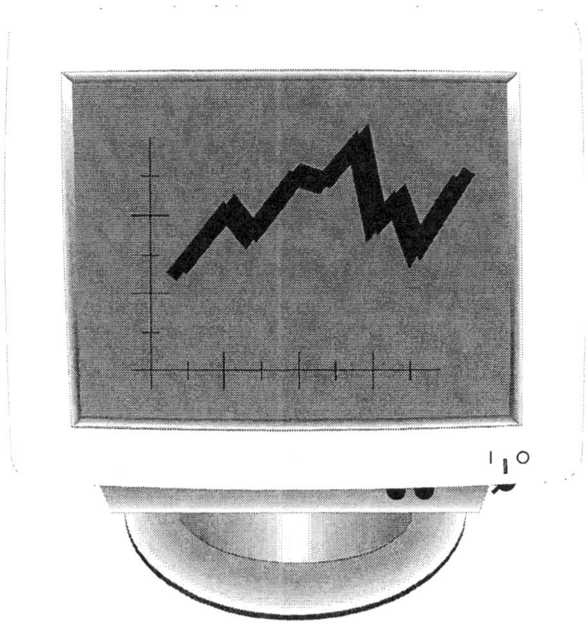

20 DAY MOVING AVERAGE

Sometimes, finding a good entry point in a trending market is very frustrating. Using the *20 Day Moving Average* in conjunction with a projected Reversal Day offers an excellent entry strategy and greatly simplifies this problem. This chapter explores ways to spot this pattern, as well as the possibilities for profiting from it.

20 Day Moving Average

The 20 Day Moving Average method provides a mathematical tracking tool for buy and sell signals. Simply put, this method *averages* the market prices over a period of time. When the market retraces to the moving average in conjunction with a Reversal Day, look for a confirmation signal.

This signal is a quick and powerful means to establish the end of a retracement. With this method, once the retracement is identified, we know the market is likely to resume the original trend.

<u>To determine the 20 Day Moving Average do the following:</u>

1. Take the last 20 closing prices and add them up
2. Divide them by 20.
3. If the 20 Day Moving Average coincides with a scheduled Reversal Day, the trader should be ready to enter on a confirmed signal.

What You Should Know About The Twenty Day Moving Average

1. If a market is moving higher, a trader waits for the pullback to the *20-Day Moving Average.*

2. If the pullback to the *20-Day Moving Average* coincides with a scheduled *Reversal Day,* be ready to enter on a confirmed signal.

How to calculate a 20-Day Moving Average

- Take the last 20 closing prices and add them up.
- Divide that number by 20.
- If the 20-Day Moving Average coincides with a scheduled Reversal Day, the trader should be ready to enter on a confirmed signal.
- The next day, drop the oldest price and add the newest price.
- The sum of these 20 prices is now divided by 20. In this manner, the average 'moves' each day.

20 Day Moving Average
Example 1

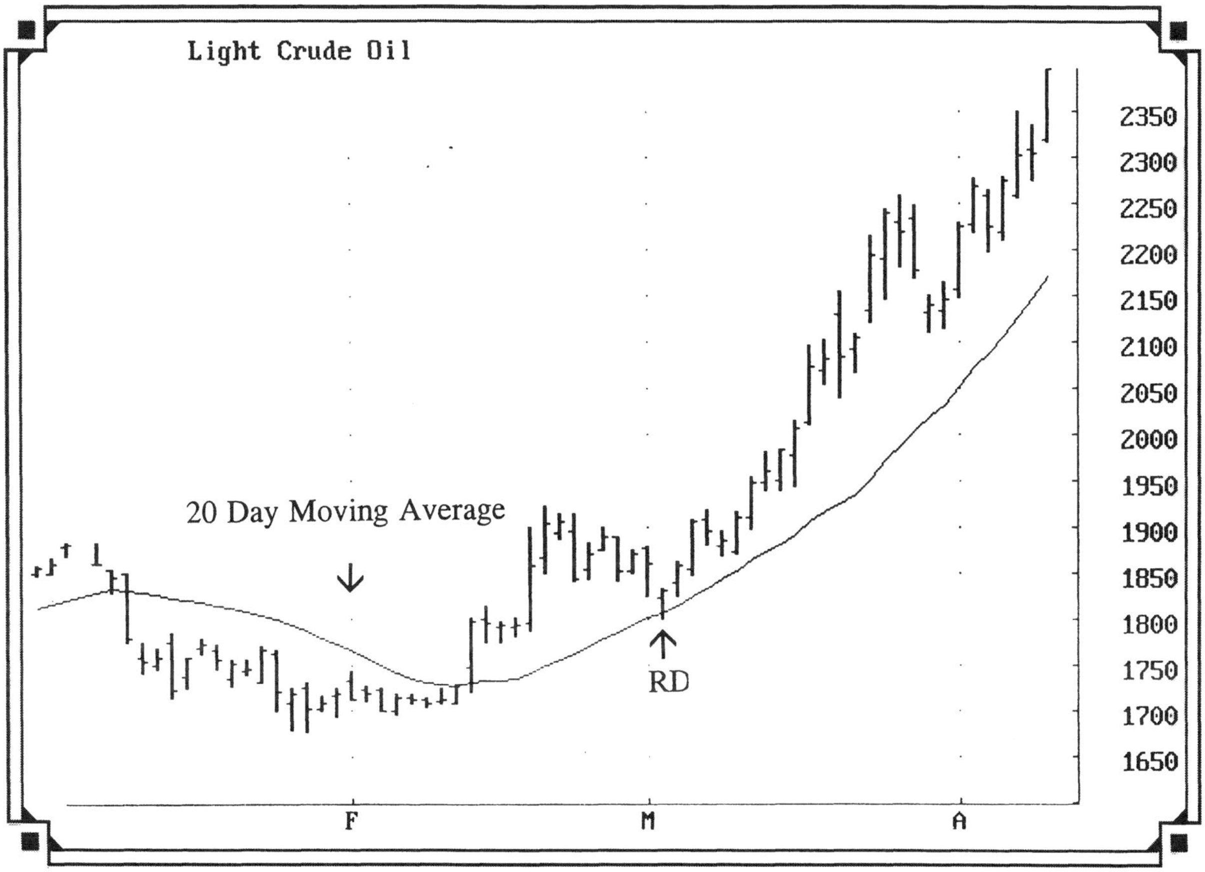

Crude Oil posted a low in late January which began a strong rally. After trading at 1923 on February 21, the market pulled back into March 4. Trading at a low of 1800, the market reached the 20 Day Moving Average in conjunction with a projected Reversal Day. This was a good opportunity for any traders waiting to buy this bullish market.

20 Day Moving Average
Example 2

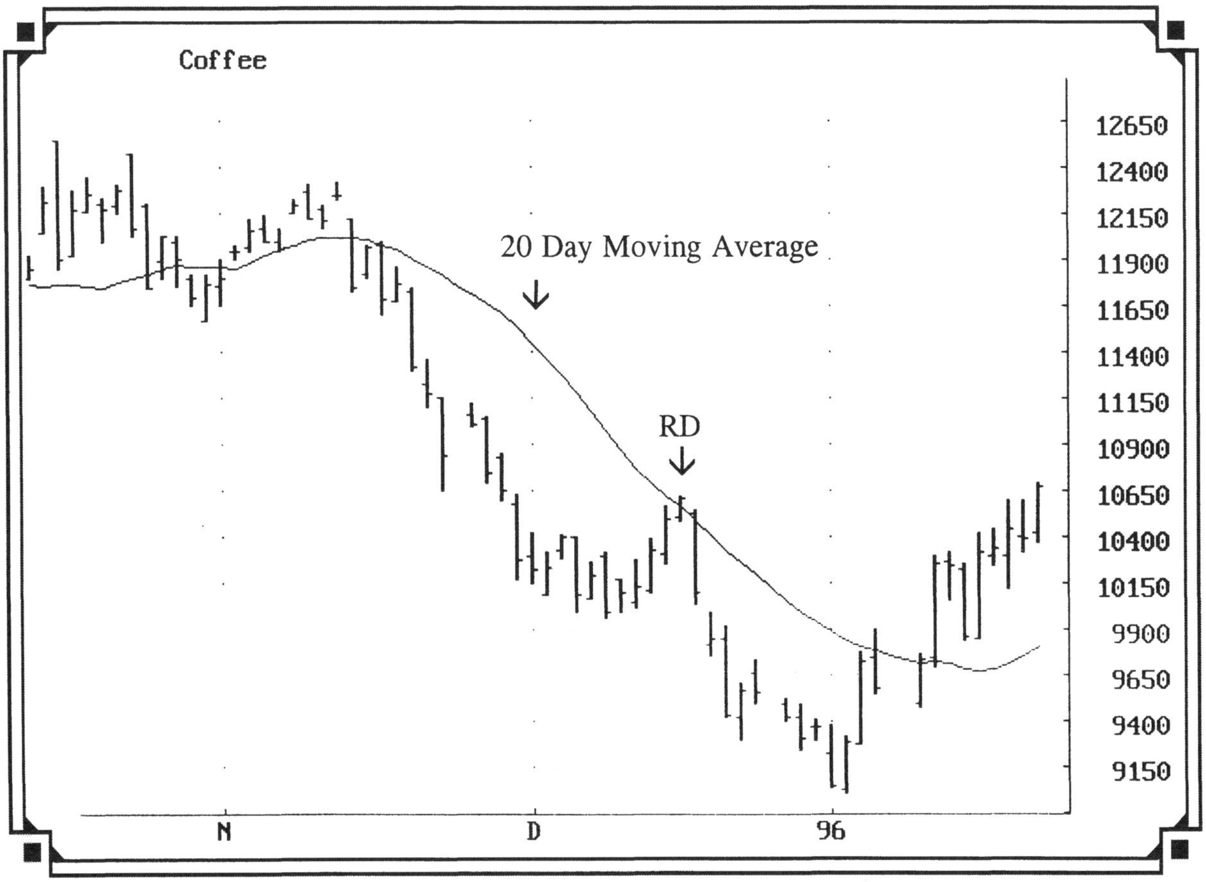

Coffee was trending strongly downward for several days. In early December, the market began to trade higher and moved into the 20 Day Moving Average. On December 15, the market reached the moving average as well as a predicted Reversal Day. Once the market reached the 20 Day Moving Average, the retracement ended. The market turned down and traded lower, continuing the original trend.

20 Day Moving Average
Example 3

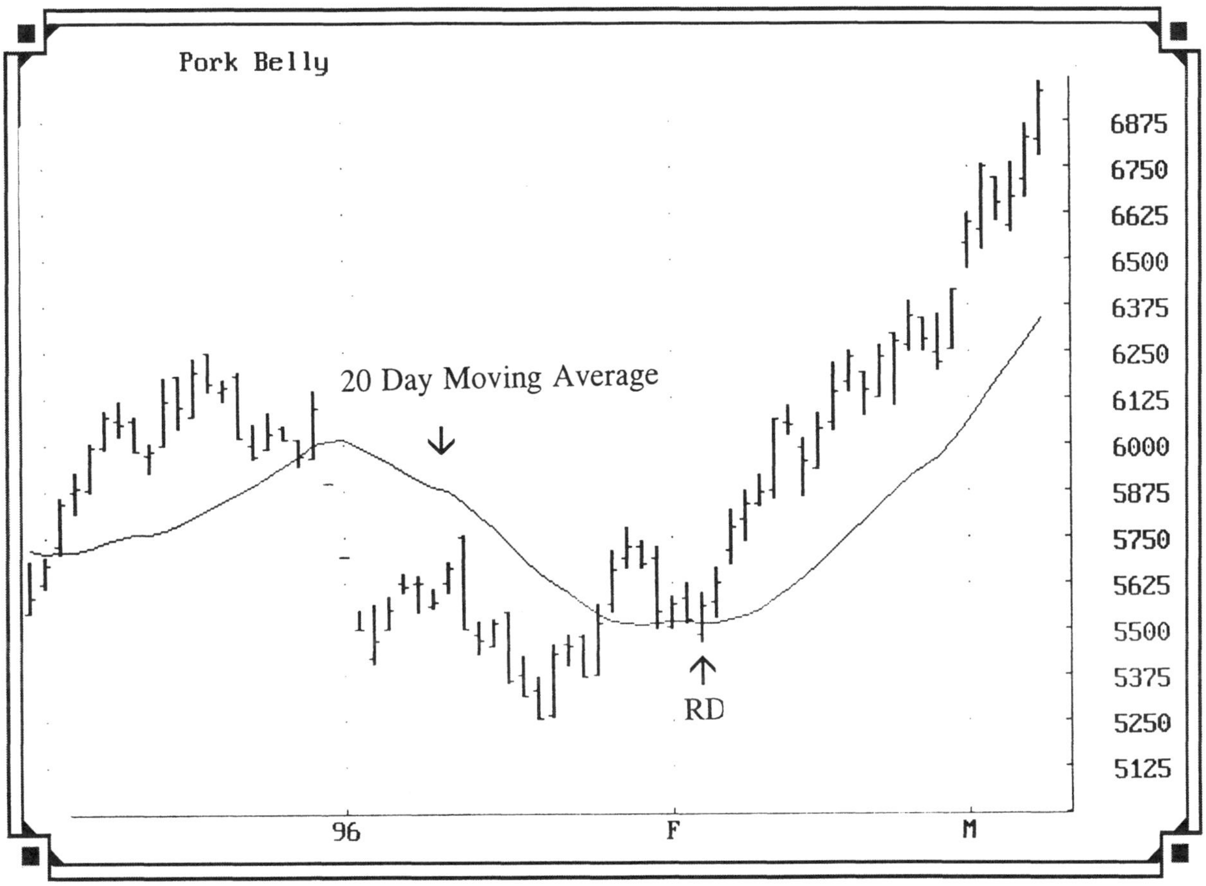

In this example, Pork Bellies hit a low on January 19 then started to trend higher. After moving up for five days, the market began to pullback. It traded lower into the 20 Day Moving Average where it stayed for four days. On a projected Reversal Day the market was sent higher and continued the trend.

20 Day Moving Average
Example 4

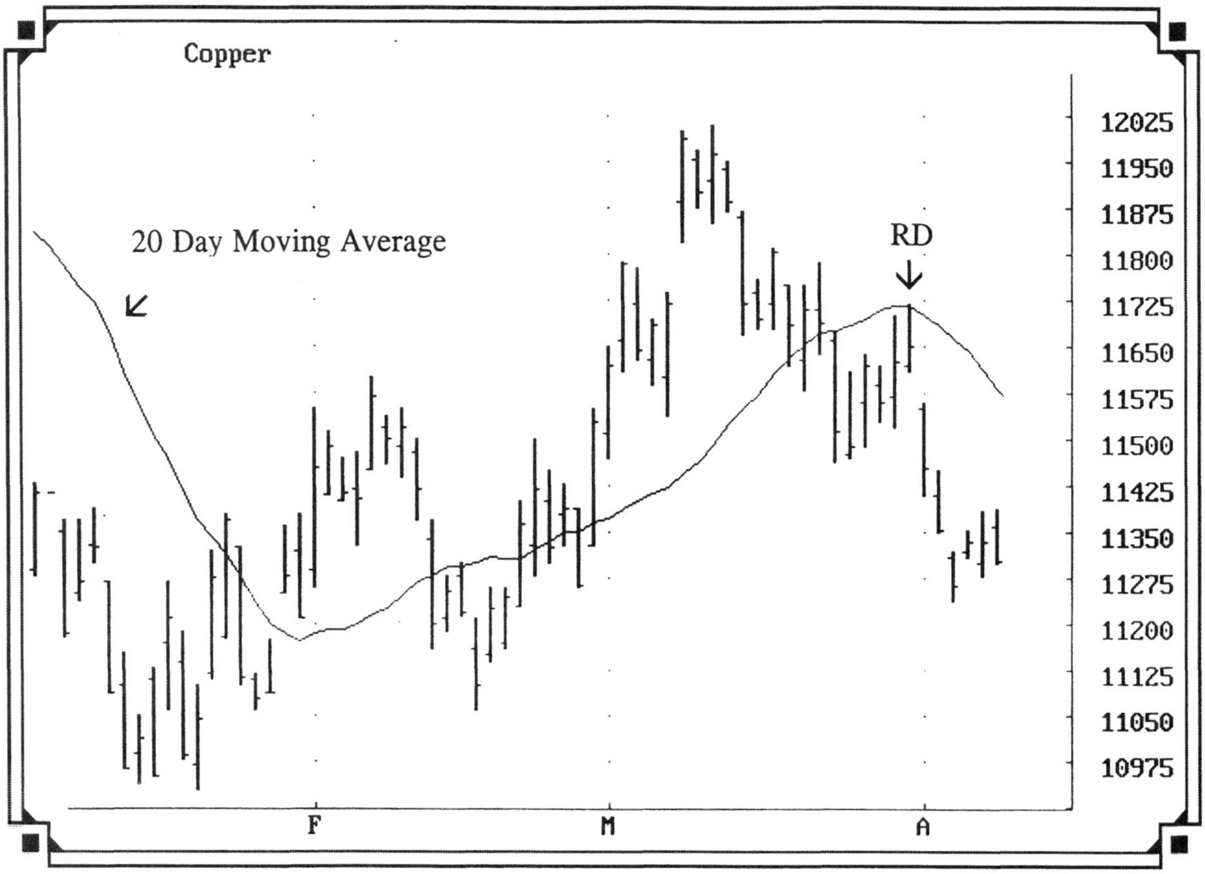

Copper hit a high of 120.10 on March 12 and then reversed to trade lower. From this high the market dropped several days before retracing. As you can see, the market moved higher into the 20 Day Moving Average and then made a sharp reversal. The market fell before continuing the original trend.

20 Day Moving Average
Example 5

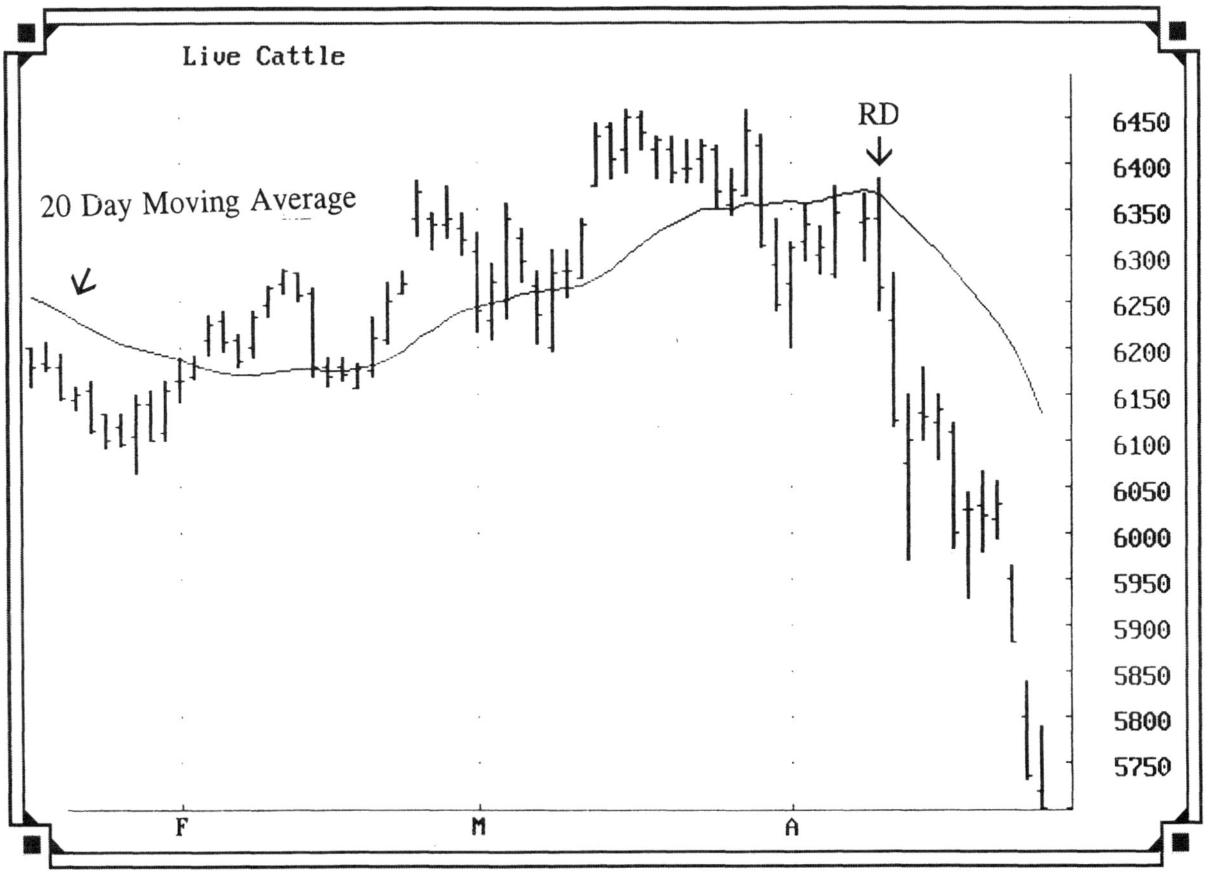

Cattle traded down through the 20 Day Moving Average before making a retracement. The market then moved higher to test the 20 Day Moving Average. Once it hit a high of 6385, the resistance stopped and sent it trading sharply lower.

Chapter 14

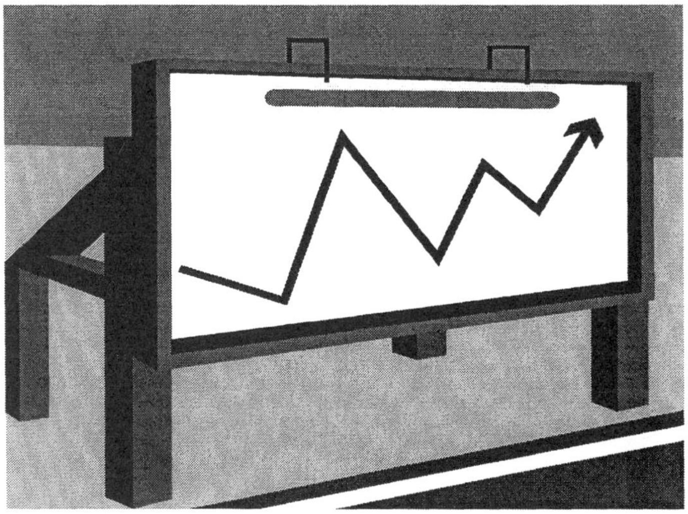

MINOR BUY/SELL WINDOWS

We now know that Reversal Days help to determine the end of market corrections. These corrections are often seen as Major Buy or Sell signal opportunities. The second kind of market correction is called a *Minor Buy or Sell Window.* The opportunity created by market corrections are quick and powerful. Once you recognize them, trading will never be dull!

Minor Buy and Sell Windows

The *Minor Buy and Sell Windows* are much like the Major Windows except, instead of a 60% retracement, we anticipate a Reversal Day in the middle of a strong trending market that retraced *only 30%.* The market correction will usually last 2.5 or 3 days *before it reverses to continue the original trend.*

The move will be quick and powerful as the market reconfirms the trend. The trader may use this strategy to either enter with the current trend or add more positions. Afterward, we expect the market to make its next strong move in the direction of the longer term trend. If timed correctly, this pullback in the market can offer an excellent opportunity.

What You Should Know About Minor Buy/Sell Window

1. The rules for the Minor Buy or Sell Window are the same as for the Major Buy or Sell Windows *except the anticipated retracement is only 30%.*

2. Minor Buy/Sell patterns are often seen in the middle of a strong trend.

3. Whenever the market pullback reaches or exceeds this 30% level, look for a Reversal Day.

4. The market correction will usually last 2.5 to 3 days before reversing and continuing the original trend.

5. Usually, a quick and more powerful move will follow as the market reconfirms the trend.

How to calculate a Minor Buy/Sell Window:

- Once a market establishes an intermediate high and starts to move lower from this high, subtract the low (beginning of the upward trend) from the high. This equals the total range of the original move.
- Now multiply the range by 30%.
- Subtract that total from the high.
- This equals the price level at which the *Buy Window* begins.

(Rules are reversed for a Sell Window)

Minor Sell Window
Example 1

In the first example, you can see two examples of the Minor Sell Window.

T-Bonds reached a high of 120-15 on February 13 (A). The market then traded lower into February 29 and made a low of 113-14 (B). It retraced for about 2.5 days. On March 4, it made a high of 116-07 (C). This pattern indicated a Minor Selling Window in conjunction with a projected Reversal Day. The market reversed and fell before resuming the current trend.

Another low occurred on March 11 (D). The market began to pullback against the trend. This time, on March 27, it touched a high of 113-02. Once again, a Minor Selling Window pattern emerged and the market reversed to resume its original trend.

Minor Sell Window
Example 1

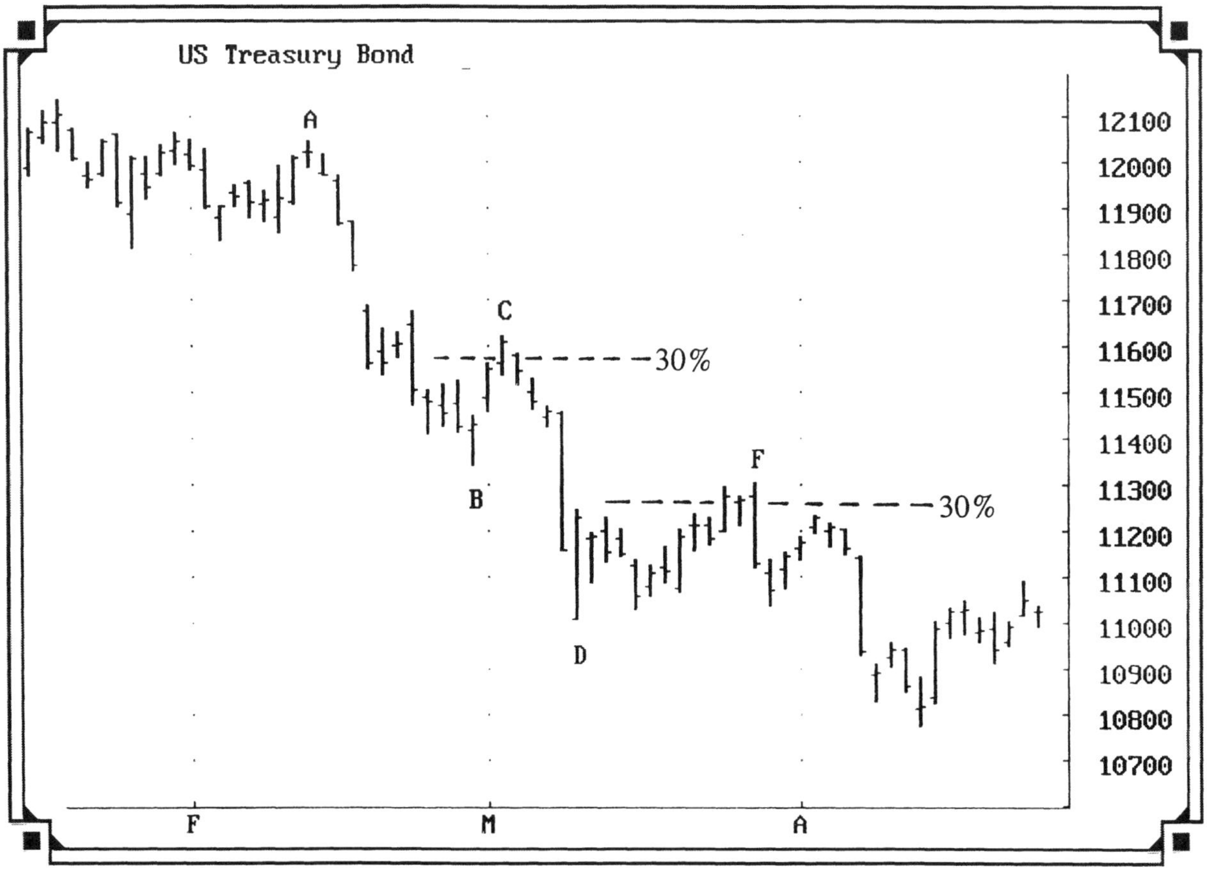

Minor Sell Window
Example 2

This second example with Pork Bellies illustrates two Minor Selling Windows. The Bellies made a contract high of 64.80 (A) on October 17. After this contract high, the market turned lower. On October 24 (B), the market hit a low of 60.50. A retracement followed and carried the market higher into October 30 (C), where it made a high of 62.50. This price confirmed the Minor Selling Window pattern as it made a sharp turn around.

Once again, after posting a low of 57.22 (D), Pork Bellies moved higher into another Minor Sell Window. The market again made a high of 59.75 (E) on November 13, followed by still another sharp decline.

Minor Sell Window
Example 2

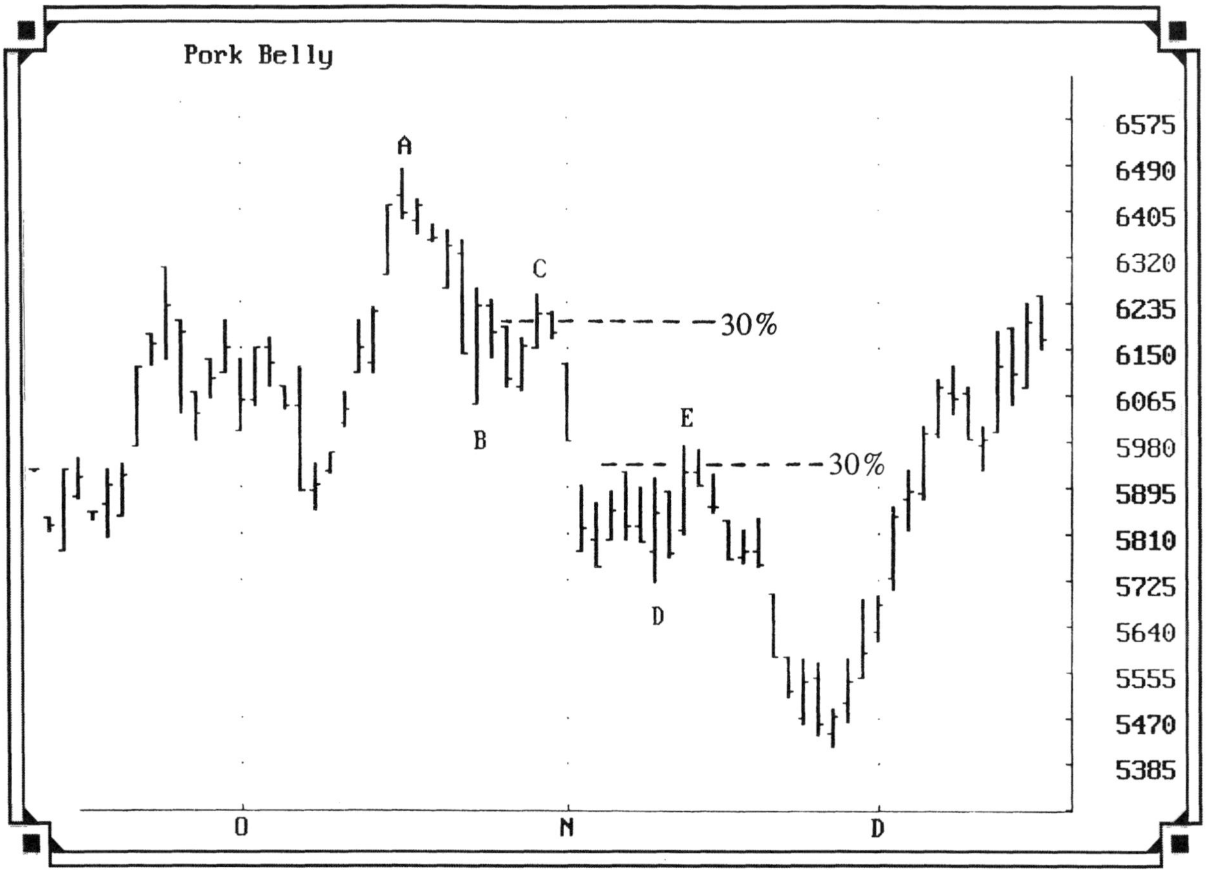

Minor Buy Window
Example 1

The first example on the next page demonstrates a Minor Buy Window. After a low of 1.930 (A) on February 20, Natural Gas traded sideways to higher. On March 22, it made a high of 2.280 (B) before pulling back. On March 27, the market hit a low of 2.150 (C) on the open, then traded higher all day up into the close. Natural Gas experienced a low inside the Minor Buy Window in conjunction with a projected Reversal Day.

Notice how, two days leading into the low day, the market closed lower than the opening price? On the third day, the market opened lower only to rally and close higher than the opening. This pattern will often occur in combination with the Minor Buy or Sell Windows. When it does, it has the potential to be a very strong signal.

Natural Gas repeated this same pattern several days later (marked as D, E, and F on the chart).

Minor Buy Window
Example 1

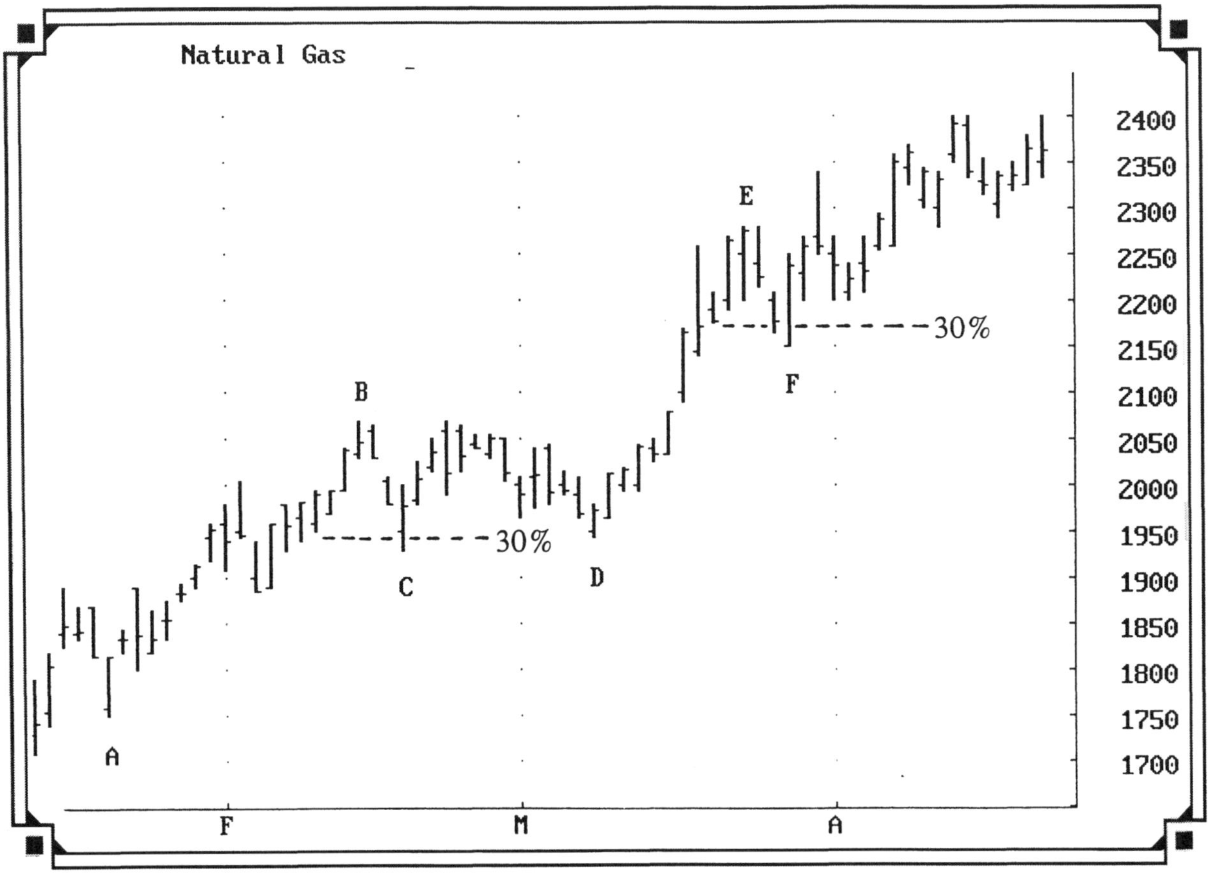

Minor Buy Window
Example 2

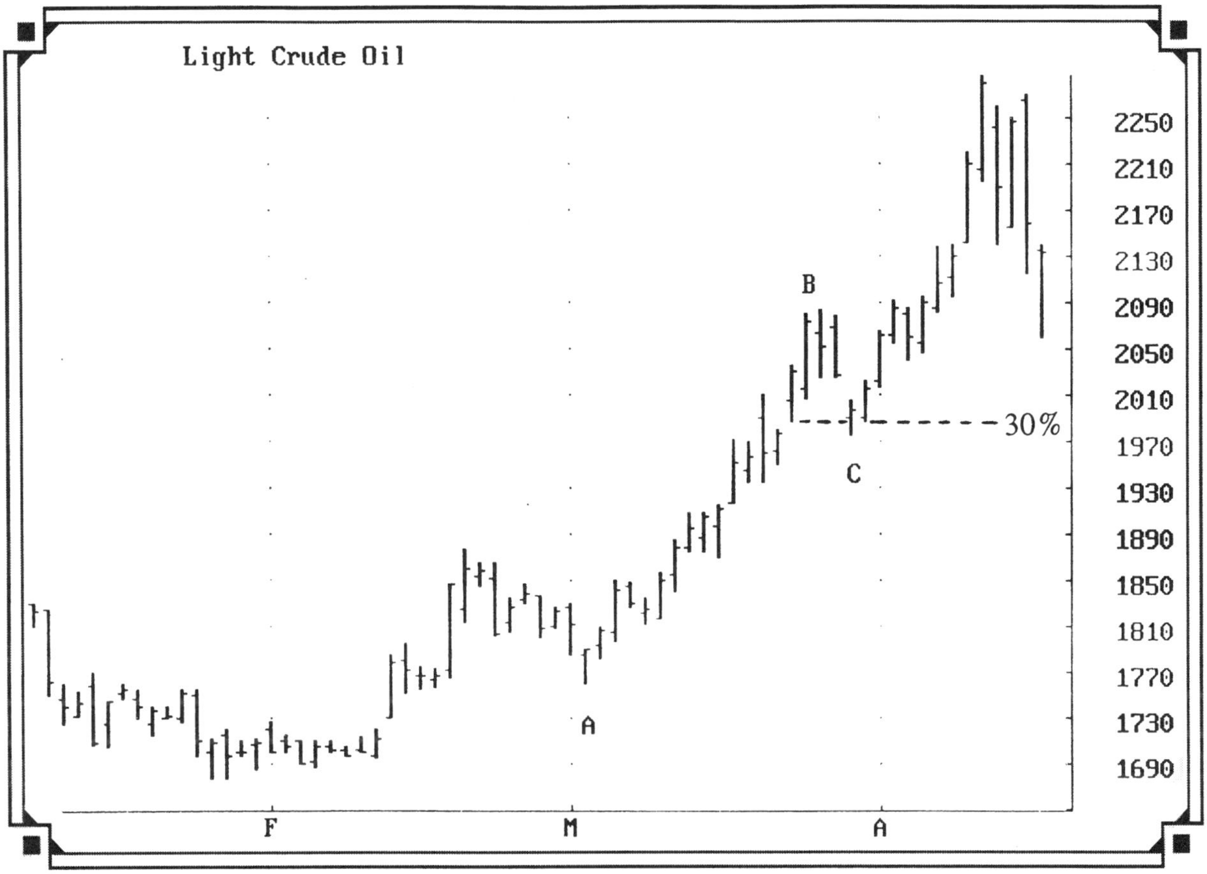

This Crude Oil chart offers an excellent example of another Minor Buy Window. The market traded higher beginning with a low of 17.60 (A) on March 4. It then hit an intermediate high of 20.84 (B) on March 26. From this high the market began to pullback which resulted in a lower close for two days. On the third day, March 28 (C), the market opened lower. The Minor Buy Window pattern emerged in conjunction with a projected Reversal Day. Afterward, the market resumed the current trend and made a new contract high.

Chapter 15

MAJOR HIGHS AND LOWS

Traders always dream of finding a way to predict a major high or low in any market. Many have tried, more have failed. This chapter explains the technique for finding these elusive signals.

When a market makes a new high/low in conjunction with a predetermined Reversal Day, look for a confirming pattern that can predict major reversals in the markets.

What You Should Know About Major Highs and Lows

1. The market must be trading higher than the high of the previous 10 market days.

2. There must be a predetermined Reversal Day.

3. The Reversal Day has to be confirmed by a Reversal Pattern.

4. Reverse the rules for a buy signal to occur at a major bottom.

Major Low
Example 1

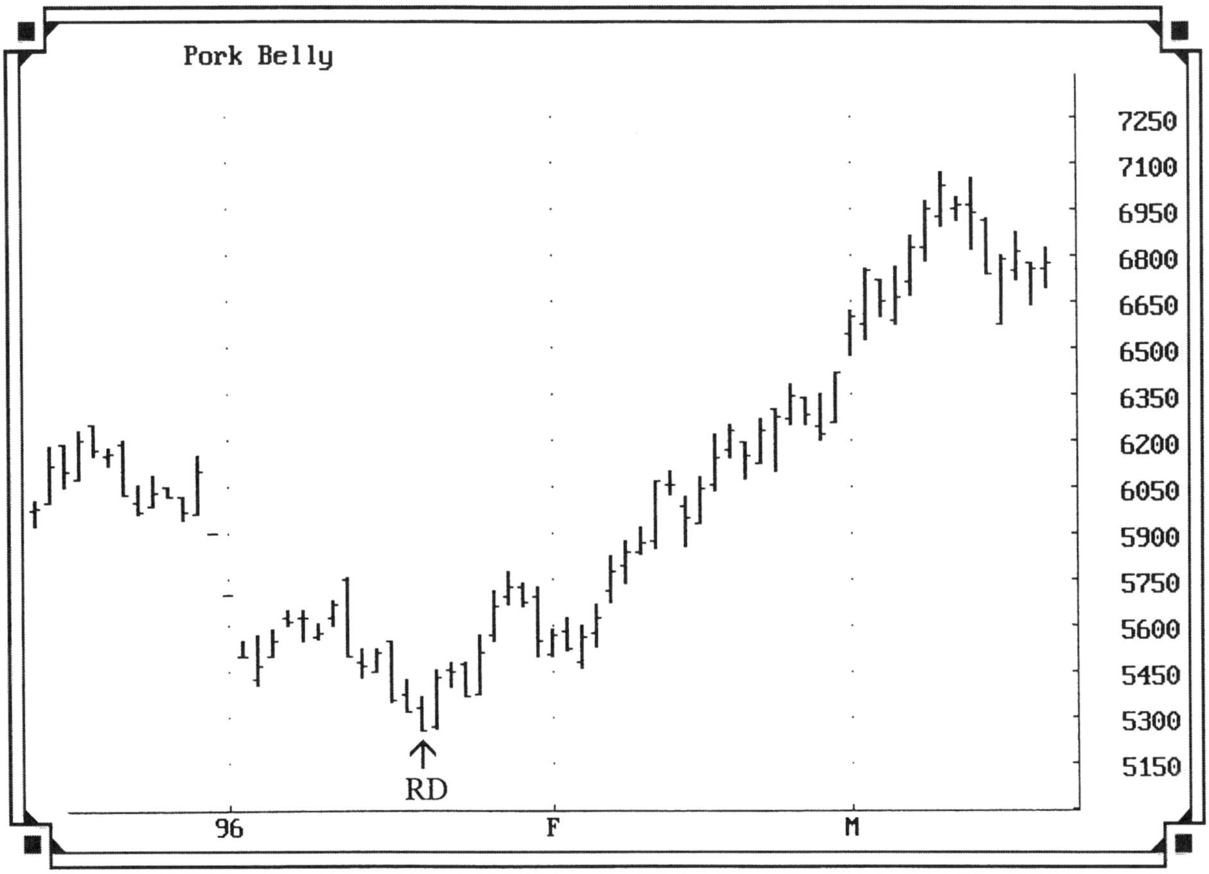

This chart shows Pork Bellies at the end of a long-term downward trend. After a short correction, the market pushed to new lows. Notice the price pattern at the low? For three days in a row, the market closed lower than the opening price. The last day is a projected Reversal Day. The following day, Trail Day, the market traded higher than the previous day's high, confirming a buy signal. The market continued to trade higher for the next several weeks. The low of the Reversal Day holds.

Major Low
Example 2

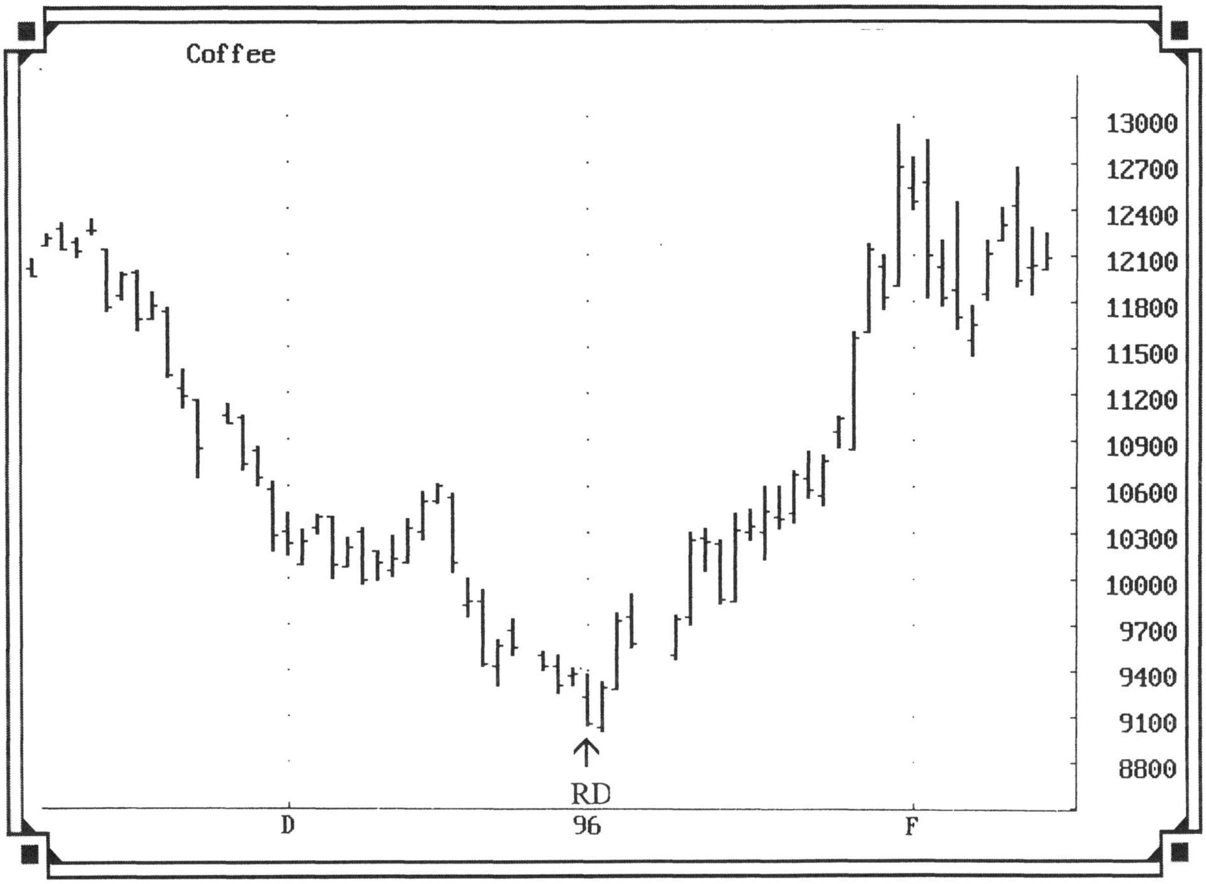

Coffee traded lower into the new year. Our projections indicated that January 2 should be a Reversal Day. As the market approached the Reversal Day, the setup patterns failed to materialize and we knew the Trail Day would have to determine the market direction. On January 3, (Trail Day), the market opened lower then traded higher all day. The market closed higher than the opening price which confirmed a buy signal to go long at the close. From this low, the market traded higher for the next month with only small pullbacks. The low established on the Trail Day held.

Major High
Example 1

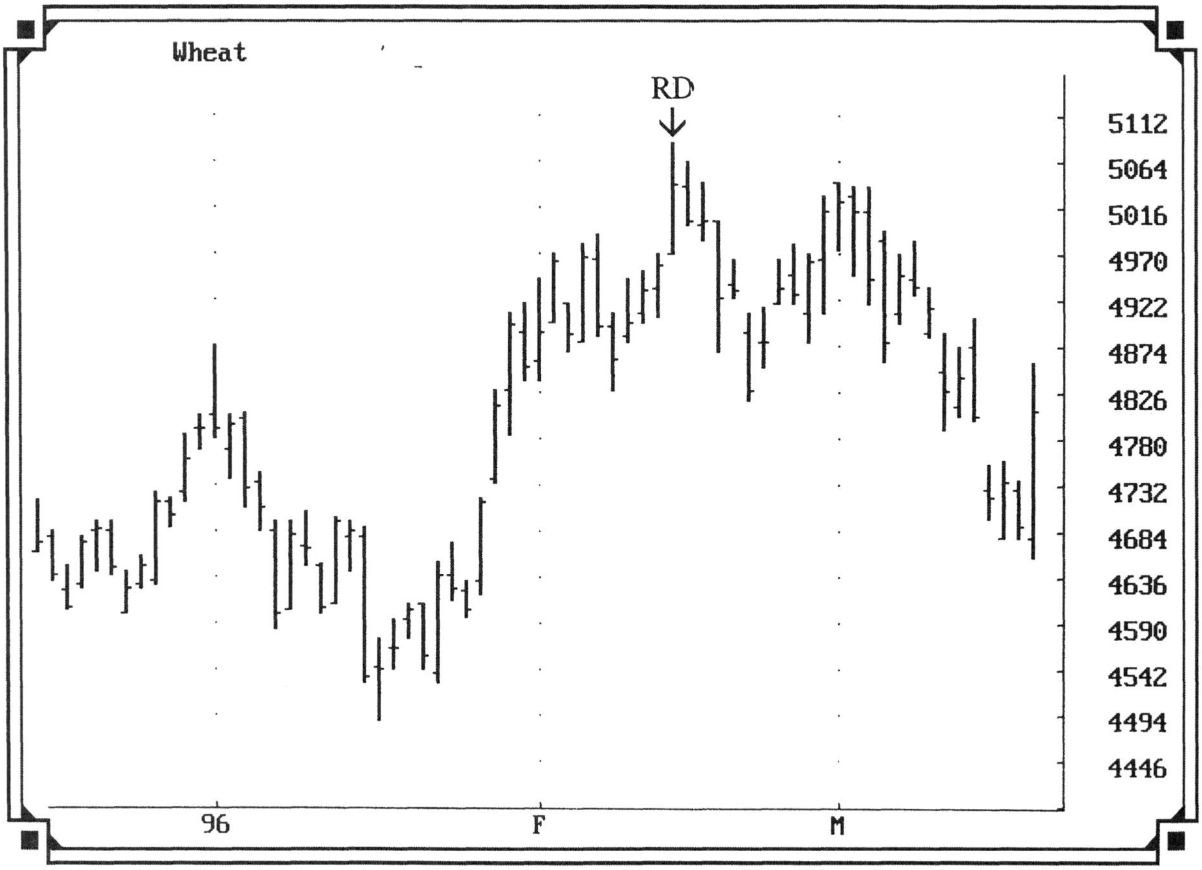

Wheat made a new contract high on the projected Reversal Day of February 24. The two setup days and the Reversal Day all closed higher. This suggested the reversal should be confirmed by a Trail Day pattern. The Trail Day did not trade lower than the previous day's low, but it did close lower than the opening price. A sell signal was confirmed by the Trail Day pattern. The high of the Reversal Day held and the market continued in a down trend.

Chapter 16

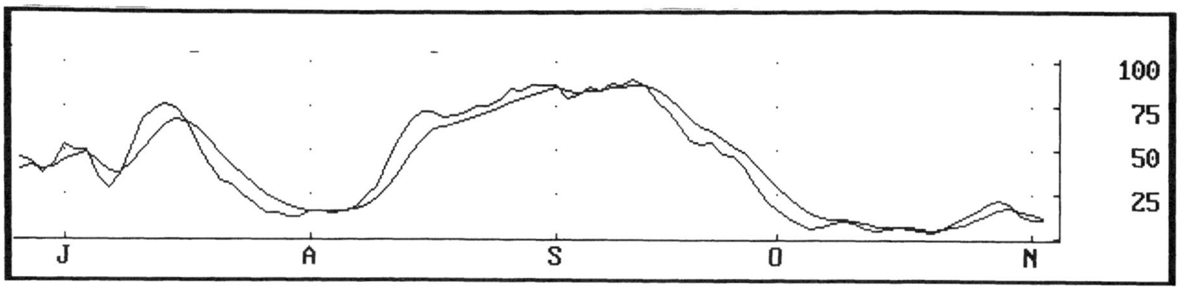

20 DAY STOCHASTICS

We feel very strongly about our Reversal Day Technique and its uses in today's market. However, we are always on the look-out for ways to improve it.

Using the Reversal Day with a momentum indicator, known as *Stochastics,* can increase the effectiveness of our confirming trade signals. This chapter describes this remarkable filtering technique.

20 Day Stochastics

The Stochastics filter is based on the theory that, as prices move higher, the daily closes should reflect the high of the daily range. Likewise, as prices decrease, the daily close tends to accumulate closer to lows of the daily range.

Stochastics calculations are based on the rate of change in the daily high, low, and close. The Stochastics chart needs two lines and three values. The three values are: the raw value, %K, and %D. These values are plotted on a scale from 0 to 100. When the raw value and %K are plotted on the same chart, the result is "fast stochastics," which shows many up and down swings in a very short period of time. When the %K and the %D are used together you have a "slow stochastic" which smoothes out the data.

Before entering a trade with Stochastics, we look for a market that has potential for a substantial move, not just a minor bounce. We like to use the *20 Day Stochastic* because it tends to smooth out many of the little ups and downs in the indicator. For your information, Stochastics can be found on almost any technical software available today.

What You Should Know About The 20 Day Stochastic Filter

1. Enter only long positions when the %K is above the %D. Remember the %K is the faster moving of the two.

2. Enter only short positions when the %K is below the %D.

3. The above rules do not apply when the %K and %D are both above 75 or below 25.

4. The market has a tendency to make major highs when the stochastics are above 75, even if the %K and %D have not yet crossed.

5. Major lows tend to occur when the stochastics are both below 25, even if the %K and D% have not yet crossed.

How to calculate the Stochastics Raw Value:

- Multiply the last close by 100
- Subtract that value by the 20 day low
- Divide by the 20 day high
- Subtract the 20 day low

20 Day Stochastics
Example 1

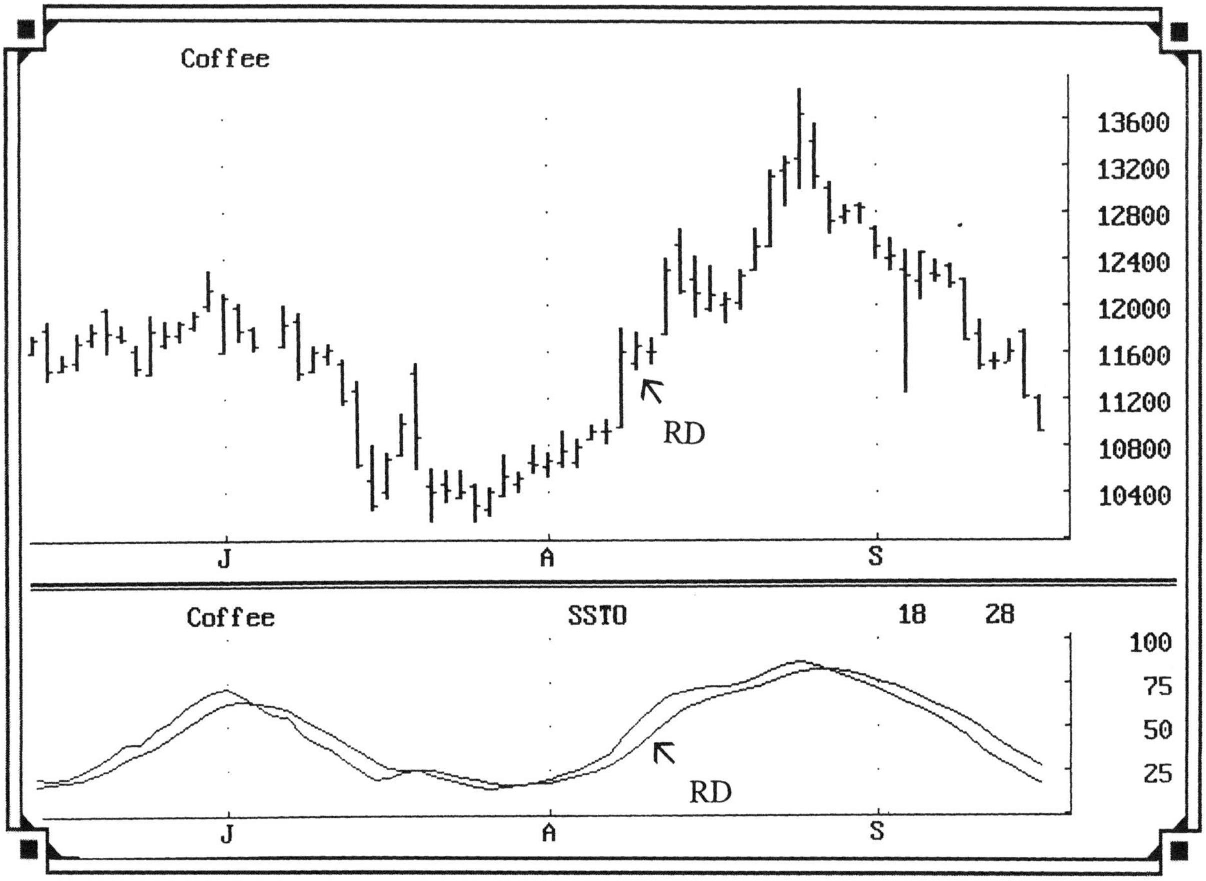

In this example, the Coffee market moved higher into the Reversal Day of August 8th. The continuation pattern seemed to signal that the market wanted to continue this trend. The 20 Day Stochastic calculation also pointed higher with the %K above the %D. Both of these two buy signals confirmed that the Coffee market wants to trend higher and thereby increased our confidence.

The Reversal Day of September 16th is another example of a continuation pattern confirming the continuation of the downward trend. The 20 Day Stochastics calculation confirmed our suspicions since both pointed lower.

20 Day Stochastics
Example 2

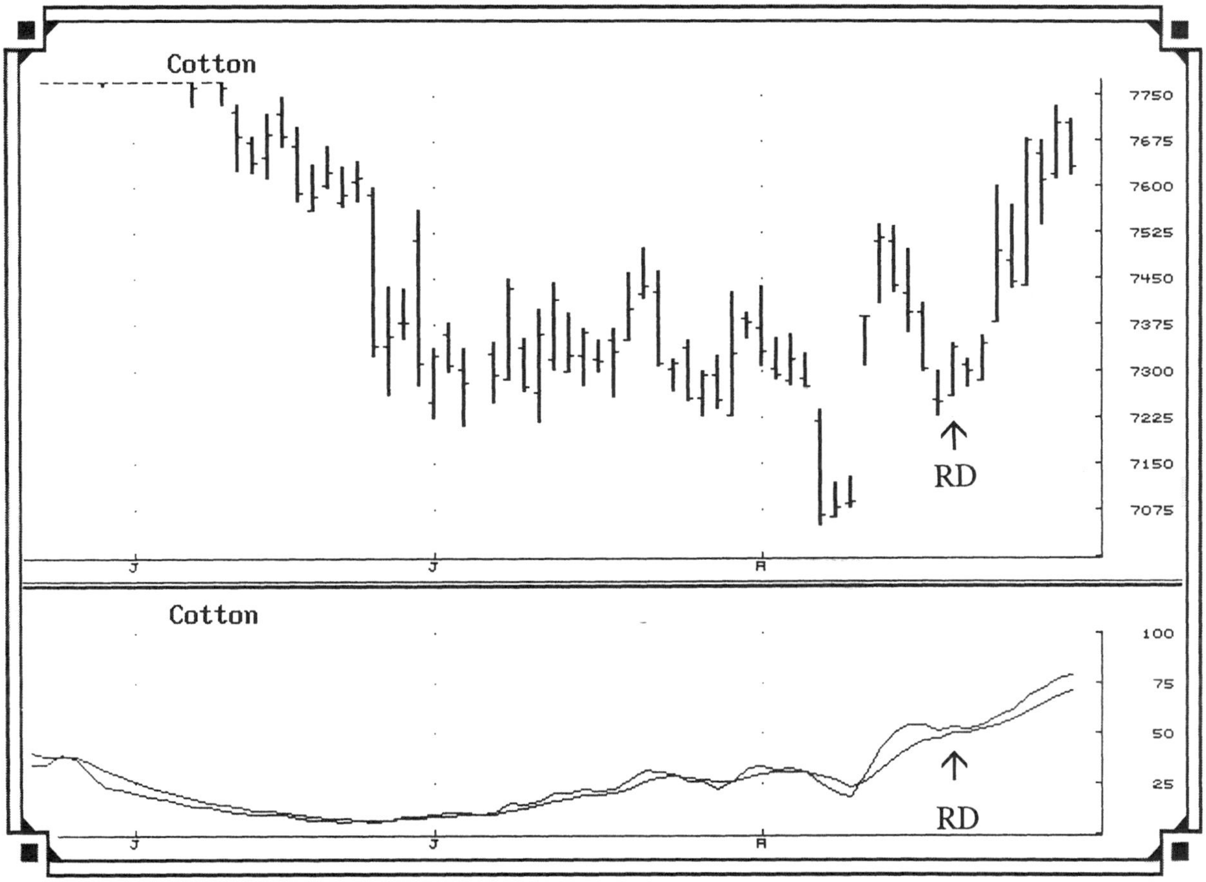

This Cotton chart shows the market trading lower into the Reversal Day of August 20. The 20 Day Stochastics also pointed higher, suggesting the trader should look only for a buy pattern. On August 20th the pattern confirmed the buy and Cotton was off for a nine day rally.

20 Day Stochastics
Example 3

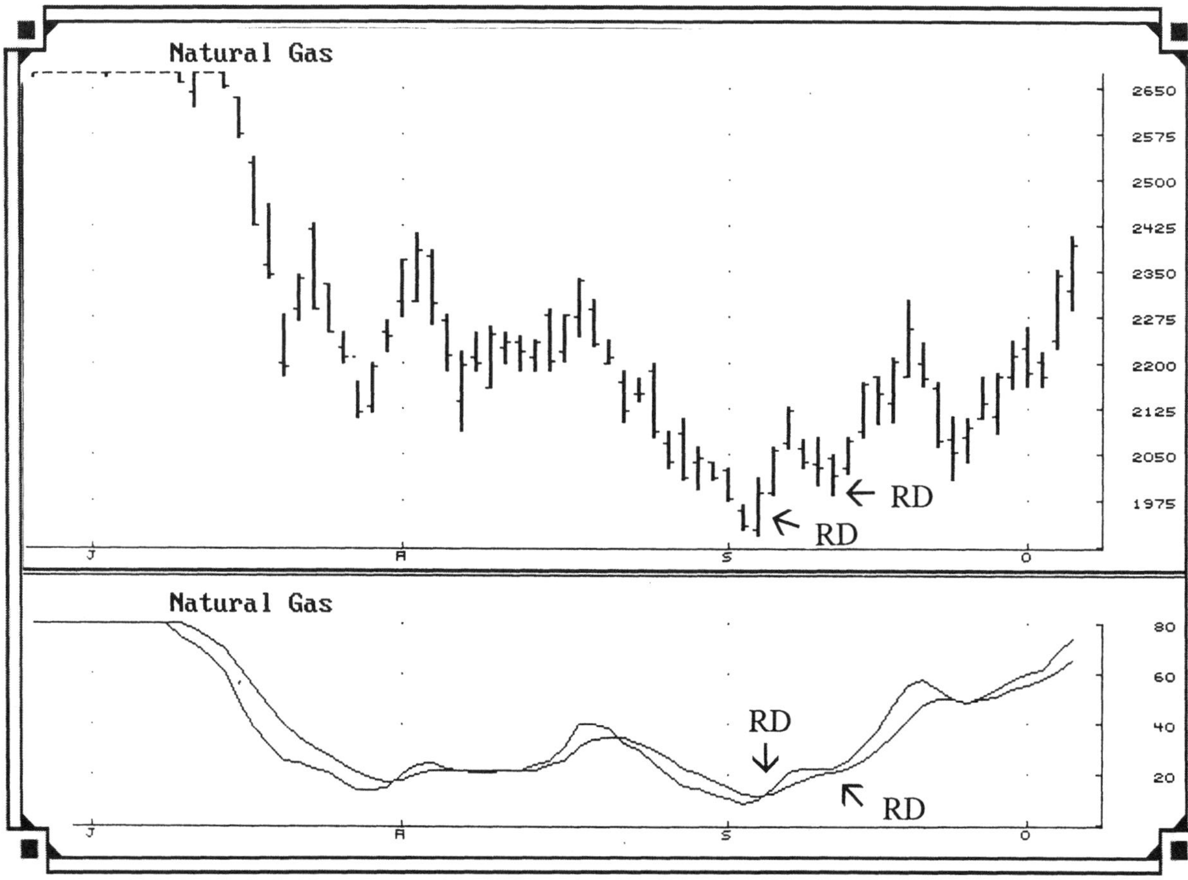

Here is an example of the market making a major low on a projected Reversal Day.

This low occurred when the 20 Day Stochastics were both below 25. Although the %K had not yet crossed above the %D, a reversal resulted in a major low being established on the date predicted.

20 Day Stochastics
Example 4

This example illustrates two trades; a continuation signal and a major bottom.

As a projected Reversal Day approached in August, the Pork Bellies traded in a consolidation pattern. A Strong Advance continuation pattern formed. The 20 Day Stochastics both pointed lower, which indicates that we should only consider a sell signal.

The next day, the signal was confirmed, and the market headed into a strong downward trend. This downward trend did not end until the next Reversal Day arrived.

On this day, the 20 Day Stochastics were both below 25. The %K just crossed above the %D, indicating the strong possibility that a bottom was about to occur.

20 Day Stochastics
Example 4

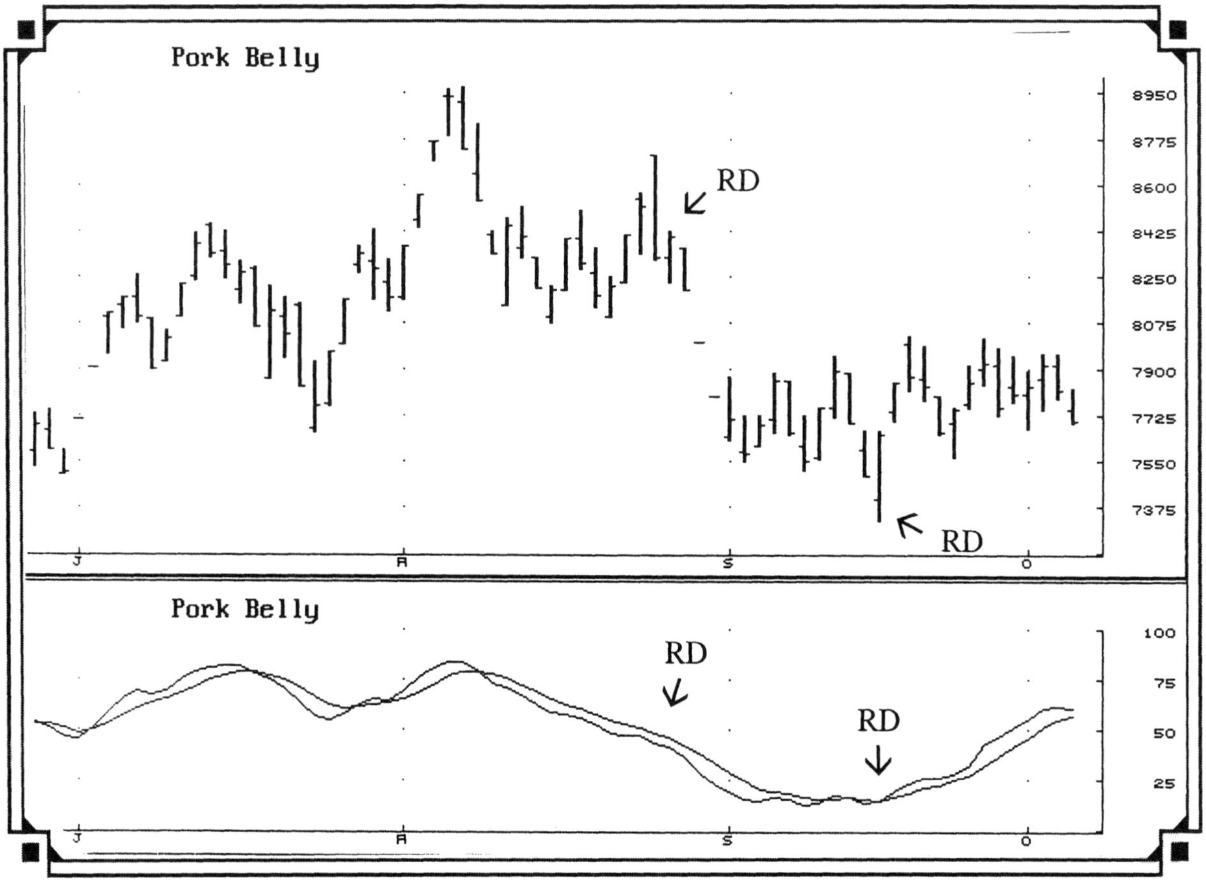

20 Day Stochastics
Example 5

After many years of using Reversal Day, we are still amazed at the accuracy of the projected dates. Example 5 on the next page demonstrates our point.

The Reversal Day was projected to occur in late June. As you can see, the market traded lower into this date. The 20 Day Stochastics were below 25, suggesting the possibility of a major low.

On the predicted date, a reversal pattern confirmed the buy signal. What followed was one of the strongest bull markets in Pork Belly history!

This higher trend continued until early August, where it ended on yet another projected Reversal Day. This was confirmed by the 20 Day Stochastics both being above 75.

20 Day Stochastics
Example 5

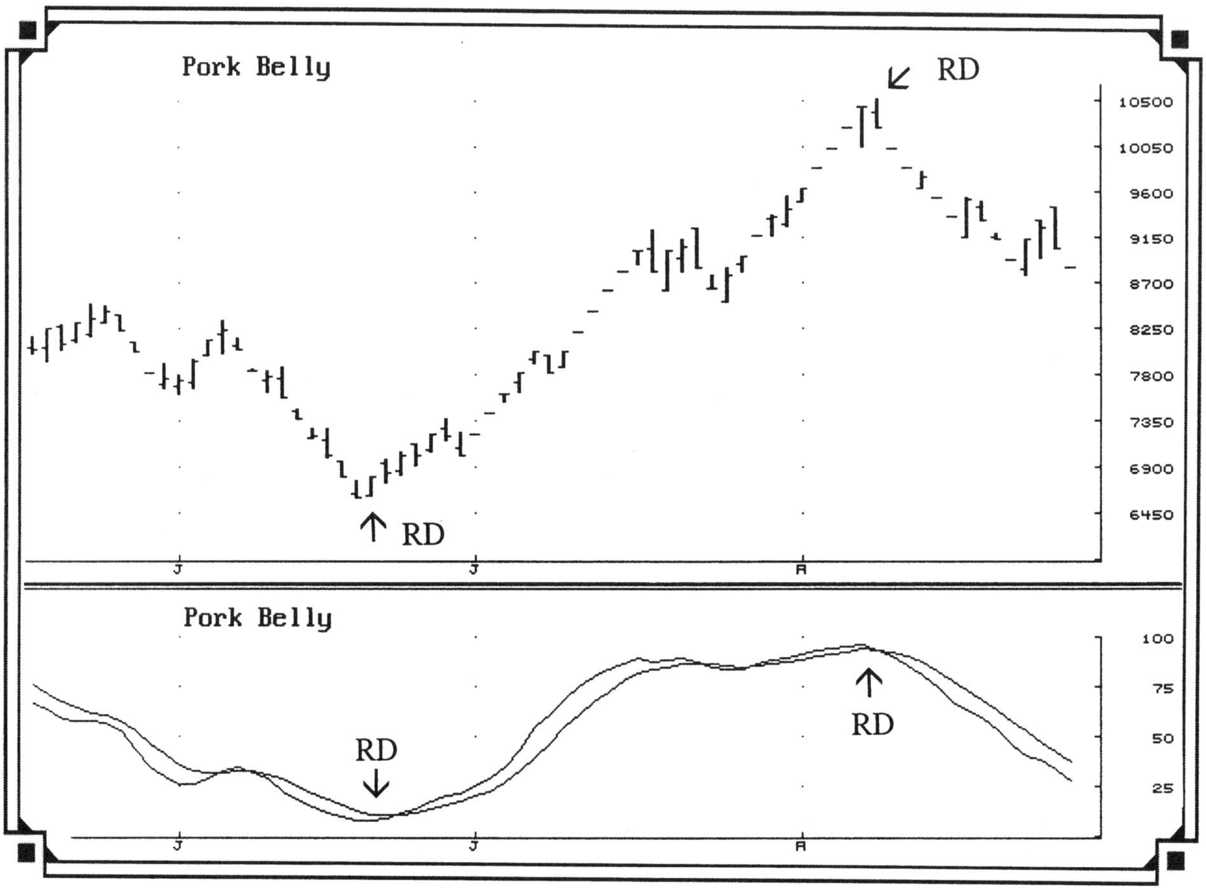

Chapter 17

DOLLAR DISCIPLINE

If the risk is not managed properly, sooner or later you will probably be out of the game. *Everyone,* even the most experienced trader, needs a risk plan before entering into the market.

By following these simple money management rules, your trading experience may be more profitable and much less stressful.

What You Should Know About Money Management

Market Diversification

There is no question, the smaller the account, the more difficult it is to make a profit. If you trade across a wide range of markets, you lower the probability of a series of losses. Therefore, we recommend opening an account that is large enough to diversify into broader markets. With the right *risk/reward ratio*, we believe that you will increase both your diversification and your odds at winning.

Stay with a Targeted Exit:

Many talented traders are no longer in the market because they refused to get out when they reached their target price. These traders not only lost their profits, but also their investment capital. It's unfortunate, but greed got to them.

Remember this market saying: ***"Bulls make money, bears make money, but pigs never do."*** What this means is, don't try to grab every penny the market has to offer. Never wait *beyond the signals,* and do not go beyond your *targeted exit point.*

Another market saying worth remembering: ***"The greatest wealth waits in the middle.***" Just because you take profits in a market that could potentially give more, this is not an indication that you are lacking as a trader. In fact, it implies that you are likely an excellent money manager. Don't be afraid to take profits!

Stay Detached

On the other hand, don't stay in the market hoping to turn a loss into a profit. Instead, be emotionally unattached to your positions and get out at your targeted point.

Always Place Protective Stops, Not Mental Stops

We have seen so many traders get caught in losing positions because they did not place protective stops on their trade. When asked why, these traders reasoned that, initially, they didn't want to get stopped out.

Big problem. Without stops it is so much harder to admit a loss. You sit there with the market moving against your position, and you wonder, when is it a good time to admit your wrong?

Most traders face this agonizing decision after getting caught on the losing side of the market without protective stops. They don't want to admit when they are wrong, especially when that error is costing money. Therefore, the temptation to wait and hope that the market will come back increases as the market sides against them.

This type of thinking is dangerous. So many times the market never comes back in time. Instead it just continues to grind against us until, suddenly, that small loss continues to grow. But, for some, even this warning signal does not turn them around. At this point, they reason that, surely, the market will come back enough to allow an exit with a smaller loss...Ironically, now they only want to get out at the small loss that a protective stop would have allowed.

However, often, the market just continues in the wrong direction until the small loss grows big and the big loss grows to huge.

Never allow yourself a mental stop. Instead of just *thinking* you will get out of the market at a certain point, place *protective stops* at the time the order is placed. This Risk Management Tool is effective for the two reasons we talked about before. Mental stops lead to greed (remember...pigs never win). Conversely, protective stops prevent you from 'riding out' a bad trade. You must approach the trade as a calculated business move, not a gamble.

Stay Positive

Don't ever get into the mental trap that this will be your last trade if you are not successful. That type of thinking touches off negative, psychological elements that will lead to nervous, pessimistic trading.

Keep track of your wins/losses:

Successful trading should *never* depend on one trade. Rather, a successful trader averages the profitability after a string of trades. Be positive and upbeat, but be willing to lose some to win more...that is the true sign of a professional trader.

The best way to keep positive and upbeat is to keep track of the win/loss record. How does it look after 20 trades, 50 trades, 100 trades, 200 trades? This record-keeping helps maintain a positive perspective and detaches you from the loss column.

Warning about Protective Stops

Once you've placed a protective stop, the pressure of the trade diminishes because it helps limit the amount of capital that you will lose if the trade doesn't work.

However, it's important to note that placing stops *does not guarantee* you will get out at the stop price. There are certain market conditions, such as when the limit moves or a gap opens, which may cause your stop order not to be filled or filled at a much worse price.

Trading Pointers

We can not advise you strongly enough on these four points:

- Do not become emotionally attached to your positions
- Use protective stops whenever possible
- Take profits the first time your target is reached
- After taking profits at the target, stand aside and wait for another opportunity to re-enter the markets
- Stay positive
- Keep track of your wins/losses

Moving the stop to break-even

After placing a protective stop, determine when and where to move your stop. The first three to four days are the most critical phase of your trade. Since the market can only do three things: go up, go down, or go sideways, we recommend you follow this plan:

1. If you are long the market and the market moves up to twice the amount you were risking, move your stop to the break even area (your entry level).

2. If the market moves sideways and is higher than your entry point, move your stop on the third or fourth day to break even.

3. If the market is lower than your entry point, don't move your stop until the market moves above your entry point.

4. If the market moves down, then you will be stopped out and live to trade another day.

What You Should Know About Dollar Discipline

1. When long the market, place stops below the lowest low of either the Reversal Day or Trail Day.

2. When short the market, place stops above the highest high of either the Reversal Day or Trail Day.

3. When the trade has been profitable for 3 days, raise the stops. Trailing the market below (above) the low (high) for the previous two days.

4. When placing stops, the following amounts should be used for the different markets:

- 40 points: Soymeal, meats, N-Gas, Gold, Bean oil
- 25 points: Crude, Cocoa, Currencies
- 100 points: Heating oil, Unleaded Gas, Lumber, O.J.
- 8 points: T-Bond, T-Notes
- 4 cents: Grains, Silver

Chapter 18

TRADING ON PAPER

Think of any profession. How important was practice? Do you think doctors need practice before operating? Does a teacher practice before that first day of school? Any professional business person practices their trade or they face months of costly mistakes.

Paper trading is practice without pain.

Caution! Go Slow...

The best advice, yet the hardest to follow, is to slow down and take the time to paper trade. Paper trading takes discipline only because we tend to dwell on the earning potential of our paper trades. However, when faced with a moment of impatience, try to remember that the markets have been around for a long time. They will continue to provide opportunities until you are truly ready to invest.

Another reason that our patience runs thin during paper trading is we tend to only remember the wins...and forget the losses. Therefore, we highly recommend you keep a record of *all the money lost and earned.* This will give you a better overall view of what real trading entails.

Chapter 19

A FINAL WORD

After so many years in the commodities business, we have seen dozens of trading discoveries cross our desks. We have been exposed to everything from books on trading programs to charting techniques that were so complicated only a computer could keep track.

Yet, after all these years and all of the different books and programs, we realize that *more* is not always *better*...and, sometimes, *expensive* just means expensive, not *superior*...

When all is said and done, we believe the Reversal Day Technique is dependable, simple, and has stood the test of time and scrutiny.

Our parting advice to you now is that you take the time to really learn the methods and then *use it.* We promise, in the right hands, this technique will enhance *any* trading method!

Evaluating Risk

Investors/Traders, should understand that there are risks associated with trading futures and options on futures. The Commodity Futures Trading Commission (CFTC) requires that prospective customers are provided with risk-disclosure statements. Historic performance results should be reviewed with the understanding that past performance is not an indicator of future results.

INFORMATION RESOURCES TO MEET ALL YOUR TRADING NEEDS!

TRADE SIMULATOR PRO

" The new standard in paper trading analysis software for Windows "

Learning to trade the markets with real money can become very expensive, but with Trade Simulator Pro, you will learn how to trade, chart, use different technical indicators, and place different kinds of orders correctly – all without costing a fortune! **Trade Simulator Pro** received the **highest overall rating** from **Futures Magazine** for trade simulation programs. Only $59.95

For a free demo you can call 1-800-831-7654

TRADERS MARKET CENTER
FEATURING " CHART BUDDY"

A complete online trading environment for beginning and experienced traders alike. The Traders Market Center is dynamic, interactive, easy-to-use, and versatile. Allowing you access to live quotes, charts, technical indicators, Commitment of Traders reports, news, trading advisors and much more. Through the Traders Market Center the trader can access their account, place orders, receive fills, review working orders and cancelled orders, etc. With monthly, weekly, daily, and five-minute bar charts, this software will meet all the needs of any trader. Only $259.00 ($159.00 with coupon.)

Sign up for the free 15-day trial and receive 30 years of historical data free!
Call now 1-800-831-7654

OPTION DYNAMICS
THE ONLY OPTION STRATEGIES YOU WILL EVER NEED TO KNOW!

One hour and 20 minutes of in-depth option instruction. Offering a simple breakdown of different eye-opening option strategies, this video explores trading opportunities using easy-to-use, option spreads and strategies. You will learn how to combine these powerful option strategies with timing methods to increase odds and risk/reward. All this for only $29.95

To order your copy call 1-800-831-7654